Brooke Foss Westcott

On Some Points in the Religious Office of the Universities

Brooke Foss Westcott

On Some Points in the Religious Office of the Universities

ISBN/EAN: 9783337036317

Printed in Europe, USA, Canada, Australia, Japan

Cover: Foto ©ninafisch / pixelio.de

More available books at **www.hansebooks.com**

ON SOME POINTS

IN THE

RELIGIOUS OFFICE

OF THE

UNIVERSITIES.

BY

BROOKE FOSS WESTCOTT, D.D.
REGIUS PROFESSOR OF DIVINITY IN THE UNIVERSITY OF CAMBRIDGE,
AND CANON OF PETERBOROUGH.

London:
MACMILLAN AND CO.
1873.

[All Rights reserved.]

ΓΙΝΕΣΘΕ ΔΟΚΙΜΟΙ ΤΡΑΠΕΖΙΤΑΙ.

PREFACE.

THE Papers which are collected in this little volume have been printed or reprinted at the desire of friends to whose judgment I feel constrained to yield. There is, I trust, a distinct unity of thought running through them, which corresponds with a deep conviction of the grandeur of the office of our ancient and religious Universities at the present crisis of national thought and life; and I should value no privilege more highly than to be able to convey what I feel on this subject to others, who may be able to regard it more completely and from other points of view.

One circumstance perhaps may lend a value to the opinions which I have expressed to which they could not otherwise lay claim. After a separation from Cambridge, for almost twenty years, I have been allowed to return to the intellectual home which I had never ceased to honour and love, and to take a part in the public work of the place. It is therefore more easy for me to estimate the real character of the changes which have taken place during that eventful period, than for those who have either watched their realization on the spot through conflicts and doubts, or now regard them only from a distance. It would be mere affectation to pretend that nothing has been lost which belonged to the ideal fulness of our organization; but it would be utter faithlessness not to acknowledge that enough is yet left at Cambridge to enable the University to exercise the authority of a true spiritual power more widely and more beneficently than it has yet done.

In this broadest aspect the work at the University must always be twofold. On the one hand, there is the work of independent research: and on the other hand, there is the work of general education. Neither of these works can be neglected without a real national loss; and neither of them can be conducted elsewhere under the same salutary conditions as are imposed by the complexity, and by the traditions of university life. At the Universities special study is guarded on all sides from the perilous temptation of degenerating into onesidedness and arrogance by the free interchange of thought; and at the same time general education is brought into close communion with manifold forms of social life.

This latter fact is at present of primary moment. It is easy to appreciate the importance of the labours of the philosopher or of the scholar or of the physicist; and there is comparatively little danger as things are now that they will be left without encouragement at the Universities. There is more fear that the humbler and less conspicuous work of the teachers of average men should be underrated. It is no doubt to be desired that the intellectual standard for admission to the Universities should be raised; but even as it is I cannot but think that the power of the Universities for good is nowhere exercised more largely than through the mass of graduates—they can hardly be called students—who would themselves find it hard to explain the subtle influences which have insensibly moulded their habits of thought and action.

The Universities indeed are not only a casual gathering of Masters and Scholars, they are bodies rich with the inheritance of a life of centuries. They sum up more completely perhaps than any other institution, not even excepting our National Church, all the past; and all the past is still energetic through them. This vital force is constantly operative even if it be undefinable. And though it may be quite impossible to determine the precise effect which the Universities have exercised upon the course of English history, no one, I imagine, would refuse to regard them as the most powerful instruments at all times for creating a true understanding between class and class, for deepening, that is, the conception of a national life, one in its most extreme multiformity. As the area from which university students are drawn becomes wider, this influence will become more effective. More new elements will be brought within the action of the old forces, and the resultant will approximate more nearly to a representation of the highest thought of the whole empire.

It would be easy to point out evils in the present state of Cambridge. The multiplication of the subjects of study and the multiplication of examinations are real though perhaps unavoidable faults. The excessive importance attached to the minutest results of particular examinations is a greater and more urgent danger. But those who are best able to deal with these defects are most ready to do so. At the same time the several Colleges are already endowed with powers adequate for successful action. And as long as free scope is given for the exercise of these internal, spontaneous forces, the highest work of the University will remain possible. But the interruption of the old vitality by external pressure, the substitution of a 'system of results,' that is of mere examination tests, for a common life, the dispersion of the corporate resources of the society, would destroy the very conditions through which this work is fulfilled.

Hitherto the changes which have been made in the constitution of the Universities, even the gravest, have been made in accordance with the wishes of important sections of their members. They have corresponded more or less with a growth of feeling within the bodies themselves, which has served to maintain the continuity of academic life unbroken. And they have been such that no one can consider them without acknowledging that the Universities are not backward in entertaining new ideas or slow in giving them a place in their system. These representative societies indeed are practically as wide as the nation itself, both intellectually and politically, and the public opinion which they embody may well be trusted to indicate future reforms when the hour shall come for them.

To mention one example only: at the present time there is a wide-spread desire that the Universities should contribute to the advancement of higher education throughout the country in some other way than by receiving resident students. The desire is an instinctive homage to the Universities, which they on their part are eager to satisfy. But this they can do only by communicating to different centres the impulse of their whole life. Their dismemberment or the redistribution of their revenues would simply maim or destroy this life which is their true endowment. Concentration and not dispersion is the secret of their efficacy; and the changes which are required to increase to the utmost their educational, as well as their scientific power, must be made in this direction.

It may be frankly conceded that the Universities have often fallen short of that which has been within their reach, but even so their success in the fulfilment of their loftiest office is written in the history of the English people. They have at least in some degree brought together and interpreted and reconciled at once the studies and the thoughts of men, and men themselves. As the problems which spring out of the relations of science, and life, and history become more pregnant with interest and more imperiously demand solution, the function of the Universities, as bodies in which all the past is brought into the closest connexion with all the present, grows of more sovereign necessity. With this prospect every one who loves them will labour to preserve them in their completest integrity, by shewing that every element in their constitution is instinct with fruitful life. And, to rise to the highest region of life and thought, no student of Theology who has been allowed to work at Cambridge in these later days will refuse to acknowledge with gratitude the increasing opportunities which are offered there for realizing the power of that final synthesis of thought and experience and faith, which is slowly unfolded through the ages, and yet summed up for us for ever in the Facts of our Historic Creed.

B. F. W.

Trinity College,
March 8, 1873.

I.

THE UNIVERSITIES IN RELATION TO RELIGIOUS LIFE AT HOME.

W. S.

Preached before the University of Cambridge on Advent Sunday, 1872.

I.

THE UNIVERSITIES IN RELATION TO RELIGIOUS LIFE AT HOME.

Ἡ ἡμέρα ἤγγικεν.

The day is at hand.
ROM. xiii. 12.

YEAR by year this advent greeting of St Paul comes to us with a clear revelation of the glories of our Faith. It may be indeed that our familiarity with the words dulls our sense of the promise which they contain. We look back perhaps with a vague imagination to some past change in which they found a partial fulfilment. We look forward with a languid hope to some future revolution in which they shall yet find their absolute completion. But this is not to exhaust their meaning. They are not for the past only or for the future. They express the law of

Christian life. Slowly as we are able to observe it, and gradually as our eyes can bear the growing splendour, the light is ever brightening towards the perfect day. In times of quiet we may be tempted to overlook the uniform progress: in times of storm we may be tempted to mistake darkness for night; but as we regard with wider vision the divine order of the world we learn patience without losing hope. If the fulfilment of the promise for which we once looked seems to be withdrawn as we move forward, the assurance that it will be fulfilled—that it *is* fulfilled—grows deeper and more inspiring.

At the same time we cannot but see that in the growth of Christendom there are times of transition, times of sudden passage, as it were, from darkness to light, from light to a fuller sunshine, partial dawnings of a new day, in which the Apostle's words have found inchoate and yet lasting accomplishments. So it was in St Paul's time: so it was at the fall of the old Empire: so it was in the 13th century: so it was at the period of the Reformation. At each of these great crises heaven was opened to its immeasurable depths, and Christ came to His people, not indeed to establish their fancies but to satisfy their wants. And if once again we are called to live and work in the prospect of another such coming of Christ, we believe that as it has been so it will be now. If we feel the cold and the gloom; if sad thoughts crowd round us which seem to quench the light in which our fathers walked; if strange shapes bar the way and challenge the prerogatives of faith: then we can take heart from the past victories of Christianity. The light of the dawn is often first seen on the summits of the western peaks; and it may be that as we look back we shall catch glimpses of the new day in which those who come after us will rejoice.

And for my own part I cannot doubt that we do stand upon the threshold of a new age. I cannot doubt that GOD in His great love is waiting in this fulness of time to make known to us something more of the inexhaustible mystery of the Incarnation. I cannot doubt that as before the birth of the new order will be accomplished in the midst of strife and distress and perplexity, men's hearts failing them for fear. But none the less I cannot doubt that we may hasten the great issue for which we look; that we may lighten the trial through which we have to pass; that we may avert some dangers and anticipate some blessings, if with open eyes and open hearts and a faith in the presence of the Holy Spirit we try to read what lies before us.

The lesson is enforced in many ways. To whichever side we turn we can see signs of the coming change. Step by step that vast silent continent, which has always been a name of mystery, is yielding up its secrets, and Africa is coming permanently within the influence of civilized powers. In India a people, before whose venerable antiquity our western kingdoms are but of yesterday, is moved as it has never been moved before with eager strivings for purity and wisdom. The first and the last of nations are seen by us to be waiting for that which cannot be far from them, if we fulfil our work. The mists in which they are folded may be thick, but to the eye of faith they are already breaking.

Nor is it otherwise if we look at Christendom. I have no wish to read my own opinions in the dark words of prophecy, or to sit in judgment upon Churches. It may be impossible for us now to foresee to what end the revolutions which within the last three years have changed the face of Europe will be guided. But we dare not forget them; and if we wish to keep a living trust in GOD we cannot believe that their present results are permanent. The tyranny of authority in opinion, the tyranny of force in life, may not yet have actually reached ourselves, but it would be irrational even if it were not unchristian to rest content with the imaginary heritage of selfish security. If we know that our faith was designed to bring into unity the free and independent action of every part of our nature; if we know that it was designed to consecrate by an eternal sympathy the various elements of the commonwealth: we must be prepared to vindicate the Truth. There is something to pray for and something to work for. We cannot accept as final alternatives for man abject superstition or open unbelief, despotism or anarchy.

It is impossible not to touch upon these distant symptoms of the coming struggle, but our own duty in dealing with them finds its fulfilment through the circumstances of our own country. And nowhere else shall we find clearer voices of warning and encouragement. The promise moves beside the peril. But for the most part, if we dare steadily to look forward, our fears are stronger than our hopes; and if I confidently point to the coming day I would not disguise the clouds which encompass its birth. Our perils indeed are obvious. Materially there is the concentration of wealth in fewer and fewer hands, while at the same time men are treated more and more as equal units in a sum total. Intellectually there is the hasty and restless striving to fashion a system of the universe by the extension of one method to all things. Spiritually there is the separation of thought from action, of philosophy from life, which ends in the substitution of a sentiment or a doctrine for religion. In other words we are threatened by the supremacy of a false standard which destroys the conception of order: by a false unity which destroys the conception of creation: by a false worship which destroys the conception of sin.

But on the other hand the thoughts which are quickened by the contemplation of these dangers, and by the endeavour to understand the causes out of which they spring, stir in us those aspirations through which wisdom comes; and, unless I am mistaken, we are already gaining livelier, fuller, deeper views of our Christian Faith than have been hitherto revealed. They may be vague, but at least they are full of light. Never before have men been brought so near to the practical confession of the solidarity of life as they are now brought: never before have they been so firmly possessed by the sense of the ultimate cohesion of all that is unrolled in long succession through the slow experience of men: never before has it been possible for others to feel as we can now feel, what is included in the communing of the individual soul with GOD. And these are Truths which are offered to us in the one central Fact of our Faith, which again we are preparing to celebrate. These are Truths able to train, to ennoble, to transfigure our actions, our thoughts, ourselves, in that more present kingdom of GOD towards which we look. These are Truths which self-restraint, simplicity and largeness of heart, warmth and tenderness of spiritual life can reveal and illustrate. These are Truths, to speak shortly, which the discipline, the studies, the friendships of our University seem to be fitted to create and to develope.

This last reflection is that which I wish to commend to you. The fewest words will suffice; for I ask you all to be my interpreters, each in his own heart.

1. It is needless then to dwell on the growing evils of the excessive concentration of

wealth. They spread far beyond the circle in which they arise. The very poorest are apt scholars in selfishness and self-indulgence. And I do not think it possible that the present state of things, by which the rich grow ever richer, and the poor ever poorer, and the mass of men surrender themselves to an imitative luxury, should continue long. We may sadly or wilfully shut our eyes to the terrible contrasts of life, but they are among us and they are active. And if we love our country, if we believe, as I do believe, that Englishmen are generous, and self-denying, and compassionate; if we find the spring of our own hope in the Gospel of the poor: shall we wait to be roused by some wild cry of numbers before we organize the ministry of love? Nay rather, I will trust that the younger among us may have the grace and the courage to use the opportunities and influences of this place as a training for their after work. Here at least we have glimpses of a lofty life, which is not dependent for its fulness on the accidents of social distinctions.

Here poverty is no reproach, and riches bring no title to superiority. In one way or other self-restraint, effort, hardness are familiar to us. It is true that, even in our body, luxury and display, poor affectations of a premature worldliness, have found an entrance. But if the old spirit of Cambridge is still present and energetic, these vices cannot either last or spread. There must be many eager for better things; and it is not too much to hope that there may be fashioned in us, by a little combination and a little boldness, the type of a simpler life, sterner and still tenderer than we have yet known, in which men shall learn not to shrink from the responsibility of command, nor underrate the nobility of service; in which laymen and priests shall be joined in the fulfilment of one supreme work; in which the consecration of the cross shall rest upon labour and upon pleasure; in which the words 'in Christ' shall be the bond of fellowship and the fountain of strength. Such a life, organized and spread, would carry with it the solution of our social problems. Such a life answers to the true conditions of our life here. Here lie together in the richest profusion all the elements out of which it can be constructed; and here is that freshness of enthusiasm which is able to fuse and to animate them at the inspiration of faith.

2. In this way our University has a social office to discharge in preparation for the future. Its intellectual office is even more unmistakable. Thought soon passes into life, and the character of the coming age can be seen already in the modes of investigation which are shaping it. The last creative movement in Europe was the restoration of learning: out of that grew the Reformation. The method and the results of physical science which are ushering in the fresh crisis, are not likely to be less operative than the study of Plato. But we have the warnings and the encouragements of the 16th century to look back upon. And if our Universities contributed then to reconcile, at least in England, continuity with change, to preserve and to reveal the essential form of the one Faith which clothes itself in

many shapes, to vindicate for the old a place beside the new, to keep men's thoughts and sympathies at their highest and widest: so it may be now. We all remember how the study of Greek was discouraged and denounced: how the extravagance of its professors gave colour to the suspicion of its opponents: how for a time it seemed as if a flood of philosophic heathenism would overwhelm the West. But we remember also that these evils were partial and transient: we remember that Christianity, studied in the very words of Apostles, illuminated by ancient wisdom, placed in its due position to the order of the whole discipline of the world, has been since seen in the fulness of a majesty which was before unimaginable. And all this is a parable. We may be amazed and grieved at the haste and one-sidedness and intolerance of many popular teachers of physics: we may sympathize with the alarm of those who confound the facts of the science with the opinions of the student. But if we are touched by the spirit of this place, we shall be lifted up to a region above all personal conflicts or interests. All Truth is ours; and we are Christ's. For him who believes in the Incarnation, it is not too much to say, that wherever something more is made known of the processes whereby GOD works in Nature, something more of the dependence of man on man, something more of the unity of our whole being, there, whether in contention or in sincerity, in ignorance or in knowledge, Christ is preached; and such a one rejoices as he looks onward beyond the storm and tumult—rejoices in the wider vision which he gains of the infinite perfection of the divine plan—rejoices in the closer sense which he realizes of his fellowship with the Saviour in Whom he lives.

3. No one will question the power of University studies to guide men to this large and firm faith. No one will question that Theology is now called to bring within its scope new thoughts and modes of thinking which have not yet been coordinated with the Faith. No one— no one at least who takes the trouble to ponder them—can question that the facts of Christianity

do deal by anticipation with the last results of speculation. But it is not so obvious how our students can be armed here against the third danger of which I spoke. It might appear that the very grandeur and vastness of the views of life opened to them would bring the temptation to linger over these, and turn them from the examination of their own hearts. The danger, I admit, is real; but in this case the character of early manhood comes to our help. Never, I think, is the consciousness of weakness and sin stronger than at that time. Aspirations are then as yet too fresh to have lost their charm; failures are not so overwhelming as to have checked endeavour. The young feel keenly what they might have done, and what they have done; but the contrast lifts them out of themselves. As years go on, we aim at less, we expect less. We learn to acquiesce in a lower standard: we grow content with poorer achievement. Our work, our inclinations, the vicissitudes of life isolate and narrow us. There is no succession to the old friendships. There is no return of the old communings of fresh resolve. But as long as youth is left us even in failure the confession of great thoughts seems to be natural. There is still an intensity of life which moves us, even through defeat, to lofty designs. The complete sacrifice of all we are and all we have continues to be possible, I had almost said easy. Many of us, as we look back to the time, my younger friends, when we occupied your places, see in that the source of all that we have been able to do, and the promise of much that we have left undone. But to you the promise assures, as we trust, a worthier accomplishment. And if there is any force in circumstances to nerve for action, the magnitude of the crisis at which you are called to take your part in the actual fashioning of the future must bring out every power. Events move now with a rapidity which will give no time for preparation when you have once taken the field. The thoughts of yesterday seem old to-day, and to-morrow they will be taken up into some wider view. But amidst all the shakings of society, amidst all the revolutions of thought, our Advent message remains sure—sure in the completeness of its one perfect accomplishment, sure in the hope of each successive manifestation of its power: *the day is at hand.*

Strive then, by the strength of that Faith, so to live, that you may be able, when you leave us, to shew to the poor a type of life, pure and lofty, which does not depend upon mere abundance.

Strive to keep open every avenue of truth without fear and without suspicion, as knowing that all partial truths will deepen and illuminate your knowledge of Him who is the Truth.

Strive to preserve clear and effectual, even when your imagination travels most widely, the sense of your own personal relationship to GOD in Christ.

This, it seems to me, our common life will enable you to do; and as you so strive you will bring nearer the dawn of that brighter day for which we are waiting and which this season promises.

No nation, no church, if I can interpret the past, was ever called to fulfil a greater work than that to which the English nation and the English Church are now summoned. There are indeed divisions, distractions, jealousies among us: there is impatience and uncertainty: there is a natural clinging to the old which is passing away: there is an instinctive fear of the new which is not yet fully known. But all these movements and misgivings are the restlessness of half-awakened life. We can bear them because we know what they portend. The Spirit of Christ is with us; and His promise leads us on, so that we can comfort one another still when the gloom is heaviest with the apostle's words: *the day is at hand.*

The day is at hand. That is the watchword of our preparation. We must be inspired with a real sense of the grandeur of the cause for which we work. It is not sufficient that we should note the course of events and meet changed circumstances by improvised expedients. We must labour from the first to gain a clear perception of the end towards which we are moving. We must know no rest till our Faith is embodied in our conceptions of national and religious policy. So shall we gain energy for our little labours by the vision of the magnificent issue to which they contribute.

The day is at hand. That is the confidence of our labours. It is not that we are receding hour by hour farther and farther from the light. It is not that the evening will close for ever over an unaccomplished task. We know and live as knowing that an age of fuller glory is coming to the world. Nations rise and fall, but the brightness of our Faith grows by an unchanging law. Every scattered ray in which we rejoice will go to increase the splendour that shall be. Perhaps we shall not see the mode of transfigurement, but we are sure that there can never be one lost truth.

The day is at hand. That is the discipline of our lives. The light of the day is the manifestation of the Lord. And that manifestation to each one of us, as to the world, is made in fire, which will consume all that is unable to bear the divine presence. If then we are severally without Christ the prospect of that day is intolerable. But if we are in Him, this thought itself, even in the sharpness of 'keen and subtle pain,' is the assurance that we shall be made like Him: if we are in Him we can offer our work to His chastening love, as knowing that He will purify and save both us and it: if we are in Him we can bear cheerfully the cold mists which go before the dawn: if we are in Him we can wait without impatience, and rest in the certainty that His will finds its fulfilment. Conscious of our own failures, saddened by evils with which we cannot cope, perplexed by uncertainties which we cannot resolve, we shall repeat one to another, with a faith which reaches from the fortunes of a universe to the destiny of a single soul, the burden of our Advent message: *the day is at hand.*

Lord, *in Thy light shall we see light.*

II.

THE UNIVERSITIES IN RELATION TO MISSIONARY WORK.

Preached before the University of Cambridge on the Second Sunday in Advent, 1872.

II.

THE UNIVERSITIES IN RELATION TO MISSIONARY WORK.

ἐπ' αὐτῷ ἔθνη ἐλπιοῦσιν.
In him shall the Gentiles trust.
ROM. xv. 12.

LAST Sunday I endeavoured to indicate some of the ways in which the conditions and powers of our life here may be made to contribute towards the solution of the social, intellectual and religious problems which even now disclose to us the prospect of a new age of the Church. I endeavoured to shew that, without indulging in any visionary schemes, we may look for the establishment of a simpler type of life among us which shall open the way to a permanent adjustment of the duties and the rights of wealth and labour. I endeavoured to shew that we must be faithless to the spirit of our studies no less than to the spirit of the Bible if we do not eagerly, and yet with watchful patience, gather within the domain of Faith every fragment of true knowledge. I endeavoured to shew that the freshness and tenderness of the first enthusiasm of devotion offer to our society the substantial promise of that Christian heroism, which, as it has been victorious in every crisis hitherto, cannot fail us in this latest trial to which the Church is summoned. Such reflections may seem to be general and vague; but the broadest view of our position is not seldom that which is also the most practical. When we look inwards on self we are apt to see nothing else: when we look outwards on the whole revelation which GOD has been pleased to make, self is transfigured into a part of a grander unity.

To-day, however, I wish to narrow the range of our thoughts. I wish to direct your attention to one section of that magnificent work which lies before the English people and the English Church: and of this to that one aspect only which belongs peculiarly to ourselves. I wish to suggest to you some considerations on missionary work in connexion with university work; to point out, as I may, how we can with GOD'S blessing supply something which is yet wanting in the teaching of the nations; how we can offer of the ripest fruits of our labours that which may become the seed of a distant harvest.

The subject is one which is brought very solemnly before us during this Advent season. The urgency and the certainty of a vast want have constrained us to combine in the sacrifice of a common supplication. An effort of charity has helped us to realize a unity deeper than our differences. And in this way we may be led to hasten the accomplishment of that for which, as I believe, a world is waiting. We are all familiar with the commonplaces on English dominion, and commerce, and energy. But the facts which they express are symptoms only and signs of that which may be. If we interpret them aright, they point to the possibilities of a spiritual office of the nation as yet unfulfilled.

It may be that times of disaster and loss will be required to dissipate the crushing weight of mere material prosperity, before we can enter upon our higher apostleship. It may be that our accumulated wealth and power will be consecrated as instruments of divine service. The future alone can shew what discipline will make our ministry efficient. But this at least is sure, and this may supply the inspiration of our lives, that by our history, by our constitution, by our catholicity, GOD has fitted us as a people and as a church to be the missionaries of the world, to be the interpreters of the East to the West, and of the West to the East, to be the witnesses and heralds of truth recognized as manifold.

It is unnecessary for me to indicate here the grounds on which this conclusion rests. They lie open in our annals. And if our endowments are unquestionable, it seems to be no less certain that the proper time has come for employing them. The shaking of the Eastern peoples is, as we believe, the prelude to their offerings of devotion. The rapid spread of the Brahmo-

Somaj, the energy of the Mohammedan revival, shew that the strivings after the knowledge and the service of GOD are growing intenser in strange religions. And the fault must be ours if any who will to do the will of GOD, who contend passionately for a closer relationship with Him, who long to transfigure their life by their belief, do not find in the Gospel of the Incarnate Word the satisfaction of their longing, the realization of their hope. The sentence stands written for our abiding comfort: *In Him shall the Gentiles trust.*

How then can the Universities, how can Cambridge, take a due part in that which as a people we have to do?

It would be unnatural for any one who has been allowed to work with the help of every appliance and every encouragement, to say one word which might appear to detract from the honour of those who have entered on untried fields; who have willingly offered, often alone and unsupported, all they were and all they had, for the cause which they had undertaken. Still the experience and the difficulties of these apostolic pioneers of faith enable us, who look on their labour from a distance, to draw some lessons for the future from their delays and disappointments; and if we can profit even by their failures, they will not have toiled to no purpose. For it may be doubted whether life has any greater reward than this, that we should know that those who come after us will find the path of truth a little more plain, the rule of action a little less tangled, than we ourselves have found it. The men who made that living way on the breach at Badajos did not die in vain.

From this point of view we may without ingratitude notice some defects in our missionary work which academic coöperation would tend to remove. There is need in it, as I am forced to think, of a clearer understanding of the old faiths, and of a livelier sympathy with the peculiar religious instincts to which they correspond. There is need of a more distinct apprehension of the social power of Christianity. There is need of a more systematic effort to evoke rather than to mould native pastorates. In all these respects, I cannot but believe that the Universities are able to take a characteristic share in foreign evangelization. And those who love Cambridge best—those who feel with the most thankful confidence that power has been entrusted to her to meet the religious wants of our own age—must be ready to labour that her peculiar influence may reach throughout our empire. Something will be gained if each solitary minister of Christ on the outskirts of civilization may be sure that he can command all the resources of counsel and knowledge which belong to this great Christian body.

1. Our missionary teaching hitherto has been, I say, for the most part too defined and traditional. We have inherited a priceless treasure of elaborated doctrine, which represents the experience, the thought, the character of the West. We feel, more or less distinctly, how every detail of it is a pledge that Christianity answers to our special wants. We know that it has grown with our growth, even if we are

tempted to overlook the present energy of the Divine Spirit by Whom it has been shaped. Our first impulse therefore is to offer exactly that which corresponds with our own position to men who are wholly different from us in history, in faculties, in circumstances of life. But in so doing we really contend, as far as lies in us, to impoverish the resources of humanity. We do dishonour to the infinite fulness of the Gospel. We forget that the value of words changes according to the conditions under which they are used; that the proportionate value of doctrines, if I may so speak, varies with the vicissitudes of the spiritual state; that our common manhood, which Christ redeemed, presents only in separate parts the whole richness of its capacities and wealth; that our essential Creed is a creed of facts which speak at once in the fulness of life to every form of life. The different characteristics of Greek and Latin and Teutonic Christianity are a commonplace with theological students; and can we doubt that India, the living epitome of the races, the revolutions, and the creeds of the East, is capable of adding some new element to the completer apprehension of the Faith? Can we doubt that the intellectual and spiritual sympathies of its leading peoples are with Syria and Greece, rather than with Rome and Germany; that they will move with greater freedom and greater power along the lines traced out by Origen and Athanasius, than along those of Augustine and Anselm, which we have followed? Orientals, in a word, must be guided backwards, that their progress may be more sure and more fruitful. If we could establish the loftiest type of western Christianity in India, as the paramount religion, and it is, I believe, wholly impossible to do so, our triumph would be in the end a loss to Christendom. We should lose the very lessons, which in the providence of GOD India has to teach us. We should lose the assurance of true victory which comes from the preservation and development of every power in the new citizens of the kingdom of Christ. We should lose the integrity, the vitality, the infinity of our faith, in the proud assertion of our own supremacy.

If then England is to aim at this highest form of mission-work, this dynamical realization, so to speak, of the hope of the nations, the Universities can fairly claim the privilege of directing the effort. Here we are bound to co-ordinate all the methods and results of knowledge. We are bound to study the course of revelation in its manifold stages, and to place each fresh gift of GOD in its due relation to those who received it. To us theology appears of necessity as the crown of all the sciences, the one light which animates them with one life. To us the Incarnation, the Passion, the Resurrection of Christ, naturally appear in connexion with the aspirations, the bold guesses, the pathetic confessions of every age. What more is needed? We have among us teachers ready to contribute their manifold experience. We have students fitted to embody in a thousand different ways the great fact that the missionary work is the communication of a life and not of a system. We look round, and the prayer of the Psalmist becomes our own: '*O Lord, how long?...Let Thy work appear unto Thy servants, and Thy glory unto their children.*'

2. But again our missionary teaching has been too individual. It has been generally isolated in its range and in its application. Yet Christianity, like man himself, is essentially social. We are charged to proclaim a kingdom and not a philosophic creed: not Truth in the abstract, but *Truth in Jesus;* Truth realized in Him, who is indeed man no less than GOD. Our message ought to go forth from a society, and call men to a society. Wherever an English community exists, there is a true missionary power for good or for evil. From this, and through this, access is opened, not to one class only, but to all. The complete embodiment of the Christian life offers a vantage ground for the employ of every gift in the divine service. A representative Church, strong with a mature life, is able to shelter without overpowering the young Church which grows up about it. The

principle holds good everywhere; but in India, where religion and life are one, our hope of permanent evangelization must lie in offering Christianity in that form in which it can cope with the deepest evils of the State. The Church alone can overcome caste, by substituting the idea of divine brotherhood for the isolation of supposed spiritual descent: the reality for the counterfeit. Overpowering as the task may seem, it ought to be faced. We must conquer India by meeting, and not by shunning, that which is strongest in it.

The question has an ecclesiastical significance of which I do not now speak. At present I am concerned only with the social power of the Christian organization; and in this respect the power of our common life here may do far more for missionary enterprise than it has yet done. Let the great questions of colonial life once take their place among us; let them be considered fairly in the light of our faith; let it become habitual to us to regard all the interests and all the charges of duty as converging to one end;

and our missionaries will find that they have allies among our sons more powerful than themselves. Our faith will be seen everywhere to be a life, and not a system—a life embracing every product of thought, and quickening every form of social existence. This is, no doubt, a very lofty and comprehensive ideal of missionary work, but it is one which ought to be kept resolutely in view. There is a constant temptation, which we all feel in one way or other, to avoid the hardest forms of the problems which are offered to us. We are always looking for docile hearers and for direct influence. After a first disappointment we are inclined to stigmatize as pride what may be after all the stern self-distrust of a sad heart. There is need of something more than the personal message of the individual preacher. And even when movement seems to be slowest the power of Christ embodied in His Church will bring patience and sustain strength.

3. Hitherto, so far as I know—and this is my third point—our missionary teaching has

failed also in this: it has been not only secondary and individual, it has been also denationalizing. It is very difficult for us to appreciate the overpowering effect of a dominant class in enforcing their own beliefs. It is even more difficult to apprehend the relative shape which these beliefs assume in the minds of alien races. If then, as I have said, we are ourselves in due time to draw from India—to speak only of that empire which GOD has committed to our charge —fresh instruction in the mysteries of the divine counsels; if we are to contribute to the establishment of an organisation of the Faith which shall preserve and not destroy all that is precious in the past experience of the native peoples; if we are to proclaim in its fulness a Gospel which is universal and not western; we must keep ourselves and our modes of thought studiously in the background. We must aim at something far greater than collecting scattered congregations round English clergy who may reflect to our eye faint and imperfect images of ourselves. We must watch carefully lest

Christianity should be regarded simply as the religion of the stronger or the wiser. We must take to heart the lessons of the first age, lest we unconsciously repeat the fatal mistake of the early Judaizers, and offer as permanent that which is accidental and transitory. We must adopt every mode of influence which can be hallowed to the service of the Faith—the asceticism—the endurance—the learning which are indigenous to the country. We must follow the religious instincts and satisfy the religious wants of Hindu and Mohammedan through the experience of men from among themselves. We can in some degree, as the Spirit helps us, teach the teachers, but we cannot teach the people. The hope of a Christian India lies in the gathering together of men who shall be, to quote the words of a native journal, "as thoroughly Hindu as they are Christian, and more intensely national than those who are not Christian." The schools through which they shall be trained may be inspired by learning, like that of Clement, or by labour and discipline, like that of Benedict, but they must be such as to bring the Faith into living harmony with the characteristics of the race. And if the Universities can, as I have tried to shew, contribute to the efficiency of missionaries by making the results of wide and ripe study bear upon the methods and the substance of missionary teaching—if they can reinforce the ranks of our true evangelists by bringing the problems of colonial life within the scope of their studies, they have in schools for a native pastorate an object of special sympathy. If any one work belongs more properly than another to our "ancient and religious" bodies, it is that they should kindle elsewhere the light by which they live: that they should be diffusive sources of spiritual vitality: that they should foster and quicken all that the past offers in every place for present use. And there is nothing that I should desire more earnestly for Cambridge; there is nothing, as I think, which would give more vigorous intensity to her national influence; nothing which would tend more to preserve and deepen that grandeur which ought to be the characteristic of her teaching, than that some school of Indian students should be formed and sustained to witness to her devotion and to represent her spirit in the East. We should gain by being brought into closer connexion with men among whom the "struggling, hard-working, hard-living scholar" is the noble ideal of the race: they would gain by feeling that they were called into actual fellowship with a centre of the religious thought of England.

To organise such a school, appears to me to be the true University mission. For it is, in some degree, to offer to God the firstfruits of the best which He has given us. There is other work to be done abroad, but the Universities should aspire to that which is most difficult; to that which calls for their peculiar gifts; to that which may consecrate, so to speak, their proper work at home. And is it too much to hope that we may yet see on the Indus, or the Ganges, some new Alexandria?

I know how many appeals have been made

lately to the generosity of our University. I have no desire to divert into new channels alms and energies which are already offered to mission work. Yet, at this season, I cannot but hope that there may be some among us to whom further sacrifice may not be ungrateful; some, who knowing what this place has been and is to themselves, can imagine no higher privilege than to communicate as they are able the fulness of her life to our Indian Empire; some who feel that the great and ancient schools of our English pastorate are essentially incomplete till they are represented elsewhere by schools through which they shall contribute their resources to the solution of new problems of religious life.

The conversion of Asia is the last and greatest problem which has been reserved for the Church of Christ. It is through India that the East can be approached. It is to England that the evangelizing of India has been entrusted by the providence of God. It is by the concentration of all that is ripest in thought, of all that is wisest in counsel, of all that is intensest in devotion, of all that is purest in self-sacrifice, that the work must be achieved. Can we then fail to see what is required of us? Can we fail to recognize what we have to give?

However unworthy I am to plead such a cause, I must speak of the fulness of my heart. I must ask, not less through the love which I bear to Cambridge, than through the sense which I have of the office of England, for your thoughts, for your offerings, for your prayers, in furtherance of such a plan as I have indicated. Others will point out far better than I can how it may be realized. It does not, as far as I can judge, call for anything beyond our means. And this Advent will have come to us with a corporate blessing, if, through the teaching of the season, our University shall be guided in such a way, to take her place in the front of Missionary work. So we shall be better enabled to feel ourselves, and to confess to the world, that all that is noble, and pure, and true, is tributary to our Faith: we shall see farther than we have yet seen, into the distant glories of the mystery of redemption: we shall gain energy from the impulse of movement, and strength from the assurance of victory: we shall be cheered with an access of life, from the overflow of the life which we have given: we shall know, and not believe only, that the Spirit of God is with us.

The need is urgent but it is inspiring. The time is short, but spiritual progress is not gauged by temporal measures. The work is arduous, but our strength is the strength of the Incarnation.

The day is at hand; and therefore a fresh glory of Christ shall follow our time of waiting: *in Him shall the nations trust;* and their hope shall not be unaccomplished.

III.

THE UNIVERSITIES AS A SPIRITUAL POWER.

Preached at the Commemoration of Benefactors in the Chapel of Trinity College, Cambridge, Dec. 15, 1868.

III.

THE UNIVERSITIES AS A SPIRITUAL POWER.

ἡ κεφαλὴ χριστός, ἐξ οὗ πᾶν τὸ σῶμα συναρμολογούμενον καὶ συνβιβαζόμενον...τὴν αὔξησιν...
ποιεῖται...

...the head, even Christ: from whom the whole body fitly joined together and compacted...maketh increase.

EPH. iv. 15, 16 (comp. COL. ii. 19).

THERE can be no doubt that the familiar image which St Paul here uses is far more significant to us than it was to his first readers. The necessary action of Christianity during eighteen centuries has enabled us to see more clearly than they could the moral and spiritual connexity of the different elements of life. The faithful study of the external world has defined within certain limits the physical laws by which man is bound to his fellow-man and made dependent on the circumstances in which he is placed. A large experience of social life has revealed, at least in general outline, the variations in form under which the same spiritual powers are manifested at different epochs, and shewn that these also are subject to their proper laws. For us the individual is no longer an isolated unit, but a complicated result of an enormous past, inspired at the same time with a personal will, which makes him a source of influence for an immeasurable future. For us the State is no longer centralized in one despotic power, but broken up under manifold governments which express, or tend to express, the characters and aspirations of different nationalities. For us the Church is no longer contemplated under the one formal type of the Old Covenant, but as a divine society, growing with the growing ages, and revealed at each crisis of history with the power needed to control its issue.

This being so, it is impossible that we should not find a deep meaning in the Apostle's words hidden from earlier generations, when we think what we are, and what we know life to be; and as we ponder them they must seem to be full of hope still unrealized. They speak to us of an unseen, personal Centre of our higher being (κεφαλή), in Whom the complicated functions of existence are harmonized, and from Whom these derive their energy. They speak to us of a divine growth (ἡ αὔξησις τοῦ θεοῦ Col. ii. 19), specific and yet multiform, which implies progressive assimilation and constant change. They speak to us of a ministering and coordinating power (συναρμολογούμενον [ἐπιχορηγούμενον Col.] καὶ συνβιβαζόμενον) in every part of a vast body whereby the whole is sustained and moulded in perfect vigour and in perfect beauty. The student of nature may recognize willingly or unwillingly the inevitable conditions by which man is dependent on man, and race on race: the student of morals may feel after that common life which is alone adequate to satisfy the wants and control the powers of the individual: the student of theology may shrink from conclusions and speculations which appear to abridge the completeness of personal responsibility on which all spiritual life is based; but here the interdependence of men is proclaimed by anticipation not as a difficulty but as an encouragement, and the idea of humanity is seen to be no longer an abstraction but a fundamental fact of the Christian faith.

So it is that I have chosen this phrase of St Paul to give a character to our thoughts to-day. To-day, if ever, the boldest aspiration is for us a pious duty. The past and the future of the great society which we are now allowed to represent command us to contemplate the highest possibilities of life; and every special circumstance by which we are surrounded, whether by menace or by encouragement, rouses us to prepare for a crisis of unparalleled grandeur. It is just fifty years since De Maistre in reviewing the future of Europe said[1] that England was 'destined to give the impulse to 'the religious movement then in preparation,

[1] *Du Pape*, p. 374 (ed. 1860).

'which should be a sacred epoch in the annals 'of the world;' and these fifty years have gone far to confirm his assertion. To fulfil it rests now, I believe, in no small degree with our ancient Universities. These magnificent societies, which are themselves the monuments of the ancient spiritual power of England, contain within them the elements of a new spiritual power fitted to deal with the problems of our own age. Nowhere can we find more clearly than in them the characteristics which mark our national endowments and our national calling. They witness to continuity by an uninterrupted life which has found scope for a healthy development through every period of change. They witness to catholicity by the records of their foundation and the large scope of their teaching. They witness to the Christian destination of all labour by claiming for every public act the consecration of a divine blessing. And that which is true of the whole body is true in an especial degree of our own society. The very Chapel within which we are gathered, begun by Mary and finished by Elizabeth, is a record of a vital power too strong to be checked even by a religious revolution. The thanksgiving which we daily offer in our Hall embraces in grateful veneration the names of men who had little else in common than active goodwill for our foundation[1]. The monuments by which we are surrounded shew that we claim as our own the philosophers who laid the foundations of modern science and marked them with the cross[2].

[1] Infunde quæsumus, Domine Deus, gratiam tuam in mentes nostras, ut his donis datis ab *Henrico Octavo*, Fundatore nostro, *Regina Maria, Edvardo Tertio*, et *Hervico de Stanton*, aliisque Benefactoribus nostris, recte ad tuam gloriam utentes, una cum illis qui in fide Christi decesserunt ad cælestem vitam resurgamus, per Christum Dominum nostrum. *Amen.*

Hervey of Stanton († 1327) was rector of East Dereham, and afterwards Chancellor of the Exchequer and Chief Justice of the Common Pleas. A suit was raised against his executors for the costly expenditure at his funeral. It was replied that he was duly buried 'more magnatum Angliæ.'

[2] The words of our representative men of science, BACON, RAY (who rarely receives due honour), and NEWTON, may be quoted:

'This also we humbly and earnestly beg, that human things may not prejudice such as are divine; neither that from the unlocking of the gates of sense and the kindling of a greater natural light, anything of incredulity or intellectual night may arise in our minds towards divine mysteries. But rather that

To realize in the present this priceless inheritance is the natural office of our University and of our College. It is their natural office, and the religious future of England depends, as I believe, upon the mode in which it is fulfilled. If we are to use faithfully all the past as the source of principles and not of patterns of action: if we are to co-ordinate every fragment of truth without suspicion and without prejudice: if we are to retain and extend our belief in the supreme sovereignty of the Gospel

by our mind thoroughly cleansed and purged from fancy and vanities, and yet subject and perfectly given up to the divine oracles, there may be given unto faith the things that are faith's.'
—BACON, *The Student's Prayer*.

'Rationes autem quibus præcipue permotus amicorum precibus cessi et consiliis obtemperavi fuere sequentes:

'Primo Divinæ gloriæ illustratio. Cum enim inexplicabilis stirpium varietas, eximia pulchritudo, mirus ordo, immensa utilitas, infinitæ Supremi Opificis potentiæ, sapientiæ, bonitatis, luculentissima indicia et argumenta sint, qui materiam hanc pro divinitate tractabit, attributa illa omnibus una agnoscenda, conspicienda, veneranda proponet.'—RAY, *Hist. Plant. Præf.*

'[Deus] omnia regit non ut anima mundi sed ut universorum Dominus... Veneramur autem et colimus ob dominium. Colimus enim ut servi; et Deus sine dominio providentia et causis finalibus nihil aliud est quam Fatum et Natura.'—NEWTON, *Principia, Schol.* s. f.

over all thought and action and being; the teaching and the impulse must be *here*. The University must claim a throne long vacant, and appear to be, what in some sense it cannot but be, an organized 'spiritual power.'

The meaning of the phrase has indeed been unduly narrowed in later times. Yet it is evident that there are two main functions of the spiritual power. It has a ministerial office and it has an intellectual office. It is charged to perform sacred duties, and it is charged also to guide opinion. For a time, during periods of transition or preparation, both functions may be discharged by the same organ; but in this, as in every case, the highest development is marked by the specialization of action. As thoughts widen, a regular clergy, so to speak, rises beside the secular clergy; and men who devote their energies to the pious duties of divine ministration are fain to look to others with ampler leisure and wider opportunities for the fulfilment of an intellectual work of which they may receive the fruits.

It has been so in past time; and yet for the present we seem to be abandoned to anarchy. No great body assumes to itself the ennobling prerogative of guiding thought by interpreting on a large scale the lessons of history, by gathering together on one stage the manifold results of observation and inquiry, by impressing upon those who go forth to labour the eternal destiny of effort. As a necessary consequence energy is misdirected, faith is shaken, and individualism cramps the highest natures. Not to improvise a solution of a grave social question on abstract principles is treated as incompetence: to suggest that no one science is absolute in its method or in its results is stigmatized as dishonesty: to strive upwards in the ministry of life from man to humanity, to the world, to GOD, holding fast each assured result, and recognizing truly the relation between the evidence and the conclusion, is condemned as mysticism. Action, even with the leaders of opinion, outruns thought. Administration is mistaken for government. Those who might be great teachers are content to be indifferent practicians. The vivifying and progressive power of counsel is postponed to the constraining force of command. Political remedies are proposed as adequate for spiritual evils. An empirical system is substituted for a disciplined life.

Now it is not too much to say that the Universities, and the Universities alone, can remedy these evils. And for this end no change is needed in their constitution: no revolution in their studies: no modification of their essentially religious character. We ask only that they interpret to our own age their history, their scope, their spirit. We ask that they teach the relativity of all human developments, as opposed to finality, and thus guide action. We ask that they teach the catholicity of study, as opposed to dispersiveness, and thus guide thought. We ask that they teach the spiritual destination of every personal effort, and of every fragmentary inquiry, as opposed to selfish isolation, and thus, not indeed consecrate being, but reveal to all the fulness of its divine grandeur.

Each of these points, clearly indicated to us in the words of St Paul, seems to claim a few words of explanation.

We ask then first that the Universities as a spiritual power teach the 'relativity' of all human development. The position which ancient languages and literature have always occupied in them is a pledge that they recognize what has been called by a profound instinct 'humanity' as the basis of their teaching. But the exigencies of direct education have a tendency to narrow the limits of this vast subject; and we have suffered, suffered grievously, from the undue contraction of the rich field of historical labour. We have lost, or are on the point of losing, that encyclopædic conception of the life and monuments of antiquity which is alone sufficient here. For purposes of elementary discipline it may be, it must be, well to concentrate attention on the details of language, and on the highest models of style. Grammatical precision and cultivated taste are unquestionably the essential foundation, but these are nothing more than the foundation of classical learning. If the University exercises upon these studies her spiritual prerogative, she will shew that the subtlest delicacies of expression, the noblest masterpieces of literature belong to and spring out of a slow national growth, and pass away in a slow national decay: she will shew that the fragments to which she directs her students *are* fragments, and can then only be fully understood when they are referred to their proper place in the organic whole from which they are taken: she will shew that form and thought have ever continued to work from their first embodiment, rising again in the crises of human progress transfigured and yet the same: she will shew that for us the value of the great past to which they witness is vital and not regulative, that the high level to which they raise us is a vantage-ground and not a place of rest, that in all and under all we must look patiently till we discern that soul of man, manifested now in this shape and now in that, which has its being and lives in GOD.

At present we are exposed to two great

dangers which this spiritual interpretation of earlier times may avert. On the one hand a powerful school of politicians aims at reconstructing society independently of history. On the other hand a powerful school of churchmen aims at regenerating society by reproducing the past. Both efforts for the time may be disastrous, though in the end they must be alike futile. In life there is no fresh beginning. In life there is no possibility of repetition. But if once we rise to the ennobling contemplation of the life of the society, of the nation, of the race: if we open our eyes to the magnificent spectacle of its rich variety and absolute coherence: if we recognize the manifold significance of the long ages which we are enabled to study, and the necessary filiation of thought on thought and act on act, attested by the imperishable records which we are charged to interpret: we shall be made strong to do our own work, and we shall be made wise. A sense of reverence will move us to the undertaking. A sense of proportion will guide us to the accomplishment. What has been we shall acknowledge to be irrevocable and feel to be operative. Antiquity will be to us as our own youth, rich in hope, in vigour, in aspiration, which mature age is called upon not to contemn or depreciate, not to vainly regret or still more vainly rival, but to fulfil with sober progress and to crown with ripe achievement.

This then appears to be the first work of the University as a spiritual power, to connect its literary teaching both in form and purpose with the whole progress of humanity. But it has also to coordinate the various departments of science. For we ask again that the University should openly recognize and teach the catholicity of study. And it may seem to some that this latter work is even more urgent than the former. It is at least not less perilous to misunderstand the relations of the different groups of facts which we are allowed to investigate, than to neglect the signs and lessons of human progress. To speak of the imaginary conflicts between 'science' and 'religion' may be humiliating, but we must face the humiliation till we have removed the misconceptions which have given to them a semblance of reality. And the character of Cambridge studies seems to me to make success in this respect comparatively easy here, which elsewhere might appear difficult or hopeless. The close juxta-position of the extreme types of science, of abstract mathematics on the one side and of historical philology interpreted in the large sense already fixed, on the other, must force us to consider the enormous differences in subject-matter and in method by which the several members of the scientific hierarchy are separated. Thus we are enabled to meet at an advantage two intellectual dangers of immediate urgency. We are prepared to reassert the right of distinct types of phenomena to be regarded as materials for scientific study, when an exclusive predominance is claimed for one type. And, again, we are guarded against the temptation to admit any one method as absolute.

Very much remains to be done in adjusting the limits of the different sciences, but with these I am not concerned now. It is enough to notice that the facts which arrange themselves round the three final existences which consciousness reveals, self, the world, and GOD, spring from different sources, are tested by different proofs, and in their proper nature can *never* interfere, because they move in distinct regions. The first group rests on consciousness alone, and includes all the results which follow from the analysis or combination of the laws of human perception and thought. The second group is subject to these, and resting on observation defines with ever-advancing clearness the relation of man to the world of sense around him. The third group is conditioned by the two former, so far as its form is concerned, and resting on revelation connects the seen with the unseen, the temporal with the eternal, the finite with the infinite. The method in the first case is deductive, in the second inductive, and in the third, if I may coin a word, adductive, for it reposes on the personal apprehension of a divine fellowship. And these three methods rightly apprehended are not antagonistic, but complementary. No one is universal; but together they bring within an intelligible order whatever man can learn of thought and action and being.

And if we view these great divisions of truth in the light of history, we shall observe at once that the verification of which they admit is generically different. The first is reducible in every case to elements which are inconceivable otherwise. The second is purely experiential, and there is no reason, as far as we can see, why the phenomena which it classifies and connects should have been of one kind rather than of another. Thus the laws under which its phenomena are included depend on observation alone, which may be capable of indefinite repetition in the less complicated sciences, or is essentially unique in sociology. And though by considering the action of certain definite forces we can construct abstract sciences which we are constrained to regard as necessarily true for us, yet in practice we can never be sure that we have taken account of every element which may modify the result; and the capacity for modification varies directly with the complexity, that is, with the nobility of the phenomenon to be examined. The third division has something in common with both the other groups: its elements are supplied partly by human nature, which at least ratifies certain moral principles, partly from experience, which shews in what way the idea of the divine has been brought home to men under various circumstances. But from the nature of the case the verification must here be personal and not universal. The judgment of conscience and the conception of GOD are progressive and relative. Both claim to penetrate beyond the present order, and just so far as they serve to realize to us the unseen and the eternal they must transcend the criteria of sense, and introduce elements not included in the constitution of our own minds.

If this is so, it follows that when we have learnt to regard the whole range of the subjects with which man can deal—whose knowledge always must be human, and not absolute—

beginning with the conditions of thought and observation, and reaching over the visible on to the invisible: when we have ascertained that each superior science as it ascends in the scale, including those below, becomes more modifiable and less capable of practical verification: when we have recognized that theology is itself a science, and religion the final synthesis of all the sciences; we shall labour on each in our own narrow spot chastened, strengthened, elevated:—chastened, because we shall never forget that we see but little out of a vast field, and work but in one way out of many:—strengthened, because we shall know that our efforts are not ours only, but represent in a great measure the successes of those who have gone before us, and prepare the successes of those who shall come after us:—elevated, because we shall see that our part in the whole sum of life, however humble, has an eternal significance not for ourselves only but for our race.

For we ask, lastly, that the University as a spiritual power teach the divine destination of labour. The subdivision of study which tends to narrow us intellectually, tends also to narrow us morally. We lose the sense of proportion, and we lose the sense of fellowship. But the remedy lies near at hand. The very speciality of our operations must from time to time force us to acknowledge that we are joint-workers in a body from which we receive infinitely more than we can ever repay. And when this idea is once firmly grasped, the peril of isolation is gone. The student rises to the dignity of a minister of Christ in humanity: work becomes sacrifice: distinctions of office as great or small are lost in the transforming glory of supreme devotion.

It is indeed presumptuous to mark out beforehand the limits of fruitful service. Experience shews us that we are poor judges of the results of patient toil. But we may claim that each worker shall be called upon to realize the social character of his work: to look habitually away from himself to the great body whose minister he truly is: to discipline his vigour by casting off all that is selfish in the choice, or in the accomplishment of his task. There is not only a tendency in the individual student to press his particular inquiries too far, but there is a general tendency to extend the sway of one science into the domain of that which borders upon it. To take only the most general examples, materialism is an invasion of theology by physics: pietism is an invasion of physics by theology. And even if there is no actual trespass, it is as perilous to study a lower subject without regard to the higher, as to study a higher subject without regard to the lower. Thus there is need, in any engrossing intellectual pursuit, of a personal discipline, and (so to speak) of a collective discipline. When once this is recognized, Theology, the science of revelation, will be seen in the grandeur of its true office; and Metaphysics, the science of introspection, and Science, popularly so called, the science of observation, will be indefinitely elevated by the introduction of a moral element into abstract study. For if it be certain that the issues of all human action are infinite, and that man, whether he knows it or not, must work for eternity: if it be certain that differences of endowment correspond to differences of function, and that in life there is absolutely no recurrence of opportunity: if it be certain that not only all action but all thought is indissolubly connected, and that science hangs on science in a fixed and magnificent order: what dignity, what devotion, what intensity will effort gain, from the contemplation of conditions which ennoble even while they alarm. The power of sympathy, immeasurably greater than the power of reason, will support labours otherwise intolerable; and we shall know with a certain knowledge that the order of which we trace thus far the growing purpose can issue in nothing less than the glorious future which it is given to faith to realize.

Thus shall we rise to the apprehension of that great and crowning unity which Scripture reveals to us as 'the end.' The study of history shews the unity of life: the study of science shews the unity of thought: the study of action shews the unity of being: unities broken indeed by man's sin, but yet potentially restored by Christ. To bring these out into a clearer and more commanding light is the highest work of education. To inspire men with the sense of their sovereign grandeur is the spiritual office of the Universities.

And for the fulfilment of the office the Universities have the means ready before them. The work is indeed, as I have already said, only the present realization of the principles which they represent. No new element is needed: it is sufficient that those which are already present should be recognized. No new power is needed: it is sufficient that those which exist should be manifested in their true activity. Nowhere else can there be found the same full combination of contrasted pursuits controlled and fostered for one end. Nowhere else can there be found the same grave harmony of things old and new, which gives life to order and stability to progress. Nowhere else can there be found the same rich variety of energy consecrated to a single work, of which the very gaps which the last year has made in our body remind us with touching emphasis[1]. Here the widest, calmest, grandest thoughts are most natural. The speciality of teaching is relieved by the necessity of culture. Education passes into life. For men, who are the hope of England, are brought under these moving influences at a time when they are most susceptible of permanent impressions. Here only, the chosen representatives of a generation meet as *men*, enriching a society of equals with their different gifts. Here only they are bound together by a common discipline and a common aim, before they are scattered to the divided duties of their lives. Here only are they able to realize on a wide scale by daily fellowship that deep sympathy in difference which is the strength of action.

In this aspect the general spirit of the Universities is of more importance than the special teaching which they afford. The spirit is the

---

[1] Rev. F. Martin, Fellow 1825, † *May* 20, 1868. Rev. W. J. Beamont, Fellow 1852, † *Aug.* 6, 1868.

life: the teaching is only one embodiment of the life. If the vital power be given, experience will supply afterwards, if need be, the materials which it may shape. But no special and later study can bring that energetic principle of unity which to be operative must underlie effort. For when once our time of preparation is over and we are plunged into the turmoil of action, it is impossible to gain that clear view of the higher relations of existence which a society like this is essentially fitted to bring out. Occupations close round us, and we necessarily exaggerate the magnitude of present cares because we see them near. Our personal interests, by the force of their importunity, exclude all larger sympathies if these are not already matured before the conflict begins. In the press of the world we lose sight of life, if the life is not within us. Therefore it is that the moral impress which is given here is of inestimable value. If the spiritual work of the University is not done at once, it never can be done. If by GOD'S blessing it is done, it spreads insensibly throughout the land with a power to cheer, to reconcile, to quicken.

It may be that a stranger can feel the grandeur of the office of the Universities more than any one who is busied with their routine. At least I have not said one word which I do not in my heart believe can be made good. My own life has been spent in the humbler labour of preparatory instruction. I have learnt what that can do, and I have learnt what it cannot do. And year by year I have felt more certainly that it must remain for the Universities to satisfy the desires which at school we can only arouse, to elevate to a range truly human the sympathies which with us are special and local, to correct one form of thought by contact with others, to consecrate all by the recognition of a common service.

An ideal may seem unattainable, but when it is distinctly acknowledged as the object of aspiration, it will be found close at hand. And, if I may speak frankly, it seems to me that the total effect of the Universities, great as it is, is not at present commensurate with the resources which they command, because they do *not* set forth boldly their highest aim. There is a moral irony in those who give the tone to them, which hides from many eyes the devotedness of the scholar's life. Forces are consumed in isolation, which if revealed together in their actual intensity would produce results not to be measured by what they have already achieved. Men *can* gain at Cambridge a lofty ideal of duty, a generous enthusiasm for right and truth, a vital sense of a Divine Spirit animating all labour, but they are not '*compelled*' to regard these priceless blessings as a natural part of their heritage which they must use or deliberately cast aside. And if I am asked how this end can be gained, I answer, without one moment's doubt, Let the Universities only be seen to be what they are, let those who animate them confess openly their deepest thoughts, and the end is gained. There is nothing visionary in the sketch of their office which I have sought to draw. I know well the influences which the

Universities contain, and the character of those with whom they have to deal, and therefore I rejoice to believe that the time is already at hand when no one will come within their reach who will not find in them a spiritual power, not 'wasting the patrimony of faith,' but enlarging, deepening, elevating the conception of religious life: who will not go forth from them to his appointed place with the profound conviction that he stands between two ages, inheriting a boundless past, and fashioning, irrevocably fashioning, a boundless future: who will not thenceforth labour with the humblest sense of the immensity of that Order of which he is allowed to regard one fragment, and welcome as fellow-labourers those to whom it is given to examine other fields in other ways: who will not be animated by the spirit of sacrifice which alone is fruitful, and by the spirit of love which alone survives all change.

There is very much in life which, externally at least, is dull and weary and mechanical: there is very much in life which brings us face to face with mysteries which our reason and our soul acknowledge to be final. But if we carry with us a vital sense of the truths which the Universities can teach efficiently, routine itself will be a heavenly discipline and doubts unsolved a pledge of a nobler future. To feel no rude discords, no inexorable checks, no passionate and unfulfilled longings, to find, in a word, peace on earth, is to deny Christ: but to trust to a harmony as yet imperfect, to trust to failure as 'a triumph's evidence,' to trust that GOD will complete what we are sure that He has begun, is to know the power of Christ's Resurrection.

And when the Universities have crowned the education of their sons with this knowledge, then will England be prepared to fulfil her mission for which, as it seems, the world is now waiting. Then will she be able to interpret and harmonize the East and West in virtue of her history, of her character, of her spirit. Then will it be known as it never yet has been known, how the power of Christ can subdue all things to itself. Then will it be granted for those who come after us to see how the whole body for which Christ died, quickened by His transforming life, increaseth with the increase of GOD.

IV.

THE UNIVERSITIES AND THE INTELLECTUAL TRAINING OF THE CLERGY.

*Read at the Church Congress at Nottingham,
Oct. 12, 1871.*

IV.

THE UNIVERSITIES AND THE INTELLECTUAL TRAINING OF THE CLERGY.

THE idea which we form of the best type of clerical education necessarily depends upon the view which we take of the clerical office. If the office were simply ministerial or priestly, it would be a sufficient external training for those to be admitted to it that they should be conversant with certain services, should have mastered certain formulas, should be prepared to fulfil with due reverence and dignity specific ordinances. But however highly we may estimate the divine grace conveyed through ordination to the Christian minister, no one of us would admit that his work is accomplished when he has discharged with the most sedulous care the routine functions which he is authorised to undertake. He is a prophet and a pastor as well as a priest.

He has not only to use in definite ways a gift committed to him, but he has also to carry forward a progressive interpretation of all life, and to satisfy the wants of the individual soul. As a representative of the spiritual power, he must make good his claim to deal with religion in its human no less than in its divine bearings. He is appointed to declare a message of wisdom as well as a message of love, to shape and co-ordinate the various elements of that which is relative in expression, as well as to maintain unchanged that which is absolute in essence. According to the circumstances in which he is placed, now one part of his office and now another will be predominant, but no part can be disregarded. His education must therefore, if it be satisfactory, include the opportunity of adequate preparation for the active exercise of all his duties. He will need an intellectual training, and he will need a pastoral training, before he can fulfil his divine commission.

Of the pastoral training of candidates for holy orders I do not wish to speak now. I have endeavoured to shew on another occasion that this can be best conducted from Cathedral centres, and that our present Cathedral bodies, crippled as they have been, can still, with some little external help, undertake it. Leaving then this part of the subject for one who will come after me, I propose to indicate some essential points at which (in my opinion) we ought to aim in the intellectual training of our future clergy. This training belongs, at least in its great outlines, to the Universities and not to the Cathedrals. I desire therefore to shew how the Universities help us to secure the results which I regard as most desirable—how (1) the general character of their teaching is perfectly fitted to produce that breadth of mental sympathy on which all highest theology reposes; how (2) the special teaching in Divinity which they supply is designed to lay the firm foundation of a historic faith. The time at my disposal renders it impossible to develop these ideas in detail, but applications of the ideas will occur to every one if they are themselves fairly stated.

Briefly, then, it seems to me that the intellectual training of our clergy must be animated and ruled by two great principles which are included in the nature of their message. Christianity is the absolute religion, and therefore the Christian minister must apprehend clearly the relation in which Christian theology as a science stands to all other sciences. Christianity is a historical religion, and therefore he must be conversant with the laws of investigation into the past. He needs, above all men, largeness of view and critical discipline. It follows, therefore, that his training must be, if I may use the term, encyclopædic in spirit, and historical in method. Let me endeavour to bring out these two thoughts a little more distinctly.

The first condition of clerical education is, I say, that it should be encyclopædic in spirit. It is, of course, impossible that every candidate for holy orders should master even the rudiments of all other sciences, before he enters upon the special study of theology. But without attaining this range, he can, at least, gain an adequate acquaintance with the grouping of the sciences, with their subordination one to another, with their principles, with the processes by which they are pursued, with the foundations on which they rest. Past history has shewn, with sufficient clearness, the disastrous results which follow from the attempt to investigate one domain of knowledge, by the method which belongs to another. And the lesson has been so far fruitful that no one now would attempt to construct a theory of the world, on general ideas, apart from experience. The limits between mental and physical science may not yet be perfectly adjusted, but at least a broad distinction has been made between results reducible to elementary facts which are inconceivable otherwise and those reducible to elementary facts which are verifiable by observation. And when this distinction is once felt, we are prepared to understand that the facts of theology, as a science, are different in kind from both, and that they are established by a peculiar and independent authority. Until this truth is seen, fatal mistakes will be made in the development of theology, like those which long disturbed the progress of natural science. There is a legitimate office for deduction in physics, but the dominant facts of physics are not obtained or tested by deduction: there is a legitimate office for both deduction and induction in theology, but the dominant facts of theology are not obtained, or tested by those methods. Deduction is limited by man: induction is limited by man and the world of sense; but theology claims to reach beyond the present order, to place us in connection with the eternal and the unseen, and Christian theology starts from the union of man with God.

It is impossible to pursue these thoughts further at present; but what has been indicated will explain my meaning when I said, that the foundation of clerical education must be encyclopædic. It is of vital importance that the young student of theology should be habituated to regard the facts which arrange themselves round the three ultimate existences which consciousness reveals,—self, the world, and God,—as being supplied from different sources, tested by different proofs, dealt with by different methods. In this way he will be guarded from countless disappointments and discouragements: he will rejoice intelligently in every effort made to extend or complete each science according to its proper laws: he will know that his own science has characteristic truths which belong to it alone; and he will know also, that these truths are illustrated and advanced by the progress of the simpler sciences which define their expression, and, in turn, receive from them a crown of living glory. The theologian who studies theology only, is really as liable to error, as unnaturally cramped, as imperfectly equipped for his work as a philologer would be who confined himself to the knowledge of a single language. It is his task to watch for the convergence of all the streams of truth, to gather every scattered ray of light, without hurry and without misgiving; without hurry, for time is to him only "the shadow which his *weakness* shapes;" without misgiving, for he knows, as no one else can know, that all truth, all light is one.

Now, we shall all feel that this largeness of sympathy, this comprehensiveness of view, this patience of discrimination, must be gained before the student devotes himself to the special study of the master-science of his life. Theology, true theology, is inspired by such a spirit; but the pursuit of theology alone will not produce it any more than the pursuit of physics or of philosophy. We shall feel also that this spirit is the natural product of the Universities. No other intellectual discipline, besides that which they supply, can present to men with equal efficiency the manifoldness of knowledge, and at the same time shew how all subserves in various ways to the same end.

The combination of representative types of study in one course, as pure mathematics, and physics, and historical philology, must force every thoughtful student to consider the mutual relations of the different members of the hierarchy of sciences, and help the student of theology to apprehend the office of his own science (the science of revelation), in its proper grandeur. It is true that recent changes have tended more and more to specialise the branches of education, even in the Universities; but at present the revolution is neither final nor fatal. All that is needed to co-ordinate studies which are separately vigorous, is that theology should claim their common service.

So far, then, nothing can be better than that the candidate for holy orders should, whenever it is possible, enter completely and heartily into the ordinary University course—that is, that he should approach his professional study through the avenue of the liberal studies; that he should have at least the opportunity of seeing clearly the position which it holds with regard to the other branches of knowledge—that he should learn, once for all, that the truths which he has to teach, the method which he has to follow, are not antagonistic, but complementary, to the truths and methods of the metaphysician and the physicist. Even if the University did no more for him than this, he could not well dispense with the teaching which places him in a true position for future work. But the Universities can do, and actually do (I speak with confidence of my own University), far more than this. They not only reveal to the theological student the general relations in which his science stands to the other sciences, but they help him to lay deeply and surely the foundations on which all later construction may repose. They enable him (that we may pass to our second principle) to seize the characteristics of the Christian revelation by directing him to the study of Holy Scripture and to the study of Church History. These subjects follow naturally on the purely liberal studies with which he has been hitherto busied. They offer scope for the exercise of all the powers which he has matured. Through these, all the fulness of life is found to contribute to the interpretation of the Gospel. Through these, dogma and ritual first become really intelligible when they are seen to answer to, or rise out of, facts. Through these, if we dare not speak of *proof*, comes that conviction of the truth of Christianity on which the intellect, as well as the soul, of man is able to rest with absolute assurance.

It cannot be too often repeated, that the sum of the Gospel is a Divine history. All that it concerned us to receive as to the visible presence of Christ, His being and His work, is contained in the apostolic writings. His invisible presence through the Spirit, is made known in the annals of the universal Church. Thus, we have primary documents in which we find the essentials of our faith; we have secondary documents in which we can observe how the faith has been apprehended, how it has been effective from age to age; and these documents must be tested, revised, interpreted with thoroughness, candour, devotion, proportioned to the overwhelming importance of their contents. I am speaking now, it must be remembered, simply of the *intellectual* training of the Christian minister; and, in this respect, it seems to me to be nothing short of unfaithfulness not to prove all things by every means at our command—both the Bible, to which we appeal as the judge of our thoughts; and the records of the life of the Church of which we are heirs.

It is not, indeed, possible that every candidate for holy orders should be an accomplished critic, but every one may be expected to know the circumstances under which the books of Holy Scripture were written—how and with what general varieties of form they have been handed down to us; in what different ways they have been regarded; when and by what authority they were collected together. It is not possible that every one should be a well-read historian; but every one may be expected to gain some acquaintance with the original writers who describe the crises through which the Church has passed—to see through the eyes of those who witnessed them the victories of faith—to study the history of dogma in the words of men, out of the depths of whose spiritual experience each formula was drawn.

The Universities, I repeat, do even now present these subjects to students more efficiently than any other body could do. There is need, no doubt, of a more complete combination among teachers, of a more careful co-ordination of successive examinations, of a more obvious progress in the course followed, of a more generous recognition by bishops of the results of University instruction; but none the less the study of the Bible, and the study of Church history are vital studies in the Universities. Men can pursue them there, not as isolated fragments, but in their due relation to all literature and all life.

Such studies may seem, at first sight, secular or literary, outside the sacred field in which the minister of Christ is set to work. But they are not so. Nothing is more wanted, in order to extend and deepen the Divine life amongst us, than the profound study of the Bible, and of the progress of the Christian society. In the Bible we have the inexhaustible, unchangeable springs of truth; in the progress of the Christian society we trace the manifold developments of the vital principle of truth through conflict and failure. He who has examined, with the most unwearied diligence, the origin of the Scriptures, who has tried by every test the words which he receives, who trusts most absolutely to their exact interpretation, has preoccupied the vantage-ground of his adversary. He who does not shrink from looking upon the realities of Church history, who dares to acknowledge the dark chaos of the deep, as well as the movement of the Spirit of God upon its face, will retain hope in every season of distraction and doubt.

It follows, then, if what I have said is true, that all who have the efficiency of our national clergy at heart, should support and stimulate the Universities in the fulfilment of the two great services which they can render to the candidate for holy orders. They can render the services which I have described, and I fully believe that they are willing to render them. They can prepare him, by a grave and varied discipline, for large-minded research and patient criticism. They can encourage him to consider the position which theology holds as crowning all other knowledge, assimilating and transfiguring every treasure of thought and observation. They can guide him to a personal and intense realisation of the life of Christ, heralded by the preparation of the law and the prophets, fulfilled now as in old time in the growth of His body, the Church. They can inspire him with a sense of the far-reaching dignity of his calling as the interpreter of the Divine counsels, as well as the minister of the Divine love—so that he will pass to the special preparation for his work, knowing that he is the inheritor of a life and not of a system, of a life which is the pledge of the unity of all that is seen and temporal with that which is unseen and eternal.

We first come to feel that religion is the harmonious synthesis of all thought, all knowledge, all action, when we see how different methods correspond to the varieties of subject-matter which fall within our cognisance. We first come to feel that Christianity is inherently exempt from the law of decay when we see how it rests upon facts which are both real and infinite.

At no time could this view of the range of the ministerial work,—this searching examination of the historic foundations of the Christian life which I have endeavoured to describe, rightly be dispensed with; but at present our most confident hope of the future triumphs of faith lies in the return to what may seem to be its first elements. Every sign indicates that we are approaching an epoch when Christianity will take a new development. Once again the rule and power of the fresh growth must be sought in the Gospel of the Resurrection; the mode and impulse in the past victories of the Church. It is obvious that the problems about which men are most deeply moved in England now are social and not individual; concrete and not abstract; questions of action and not of opinion. And if we look back we shall see that it is in this direction that we may expect our faith to assert its vitality. God, man, humanity; authority, individualism, solidarity; such seems to be the succession of idea and organisation. When the Roman empire was overthrown and a new sovereign power had to be fashioned, the energy of Christendom was concentrated for two centuries on the determination of the doctrines of the Holy Trinity and of the Incarnation. When the kingdoms of modern Europe were taking shape, and the treasures of Greek thought were again opened to the world, for a like space men were absorbed in the debates on personal freedom and justification. Now, when the political life of peoples is more widely quickened, when physical inquiries have laid open some of the subtle bonds by which we are united to one another and to the material universe, our questionings take another turn. However carefully we guard all that we have received as duly established in regard to ecclesiastical order and individual liberty, all that we have received as duly defined in regard to the being of God and the nature of man, we still find that we inquire, as others about us are inquiring, whether Christianity has any authoritative teaching on the discipline of life, the organisation of society and of labour, the intercourse of nations; whether, that is, there is a social development of Christian doctrine, as there have been theological and anthropological developments. If we believe that the Word was made flesh, if we believe that Christ died and rose again, if we believe that in Him are summed up all things in heaven and earth, we cannot doubt what the answer must be, though we may long sadly wait for it.

Meanwhile, if the student of theology can be led to see at the University, at the outset of his course, what is the scientific position, what is the foundation, what is the life of his faith, he will be prepared in some degree for the new task of construction which lies before him. He will have still to learn, elsewhere, other lessons, lessons of spiritual power; but he will have learnt that lesson which will make all those that come after parts of a vital whole.

V.

THE UNIVERSITIES AND THE IN-TELLECTUAL TRAINING OF THE CLERGY.

W. S.   7

Read at the Ely Diocesan Conference,
Oct. 24, 1871.

V.

THE UNIVERSITIES AND THE INTELLECTUAL TRAINING OF THE CLERGY.

I HAVE endeavoured to shew in the preceding paper that the training of Candidates for Holy Orders is naturally divided into two parts, and that these two parts are best fulfilled at different centres. There must be first an intellectual training, in which the student may be led to see clearly the relation in which Theology stands to the other sciences, and disciplined in the rigorous criticism of the original records of his historic faith; and there must be afterwards a pastoral training, in which he may grow acquainted with practical methods of teaching and learn to minister to the wants of individual men. The first of these finds its proper home in the Universities: the second can, I believe, be best organised by a Cathedral body. If now we confine our attention to our own University it is evident that the reconstruction of our Theological Examinations offers a good opportunity for considering the general plan on which the training of Candidates for Holy Orders should be conducted, and those parts of it especially which naturally fall within the province of the Universities. All circumstances seem to be favourable for combined action. There is, I know, in Cambridge, a most hearty desire, on the part of Tutors and Professors, to unite in providing efficient instruction in all the subjects which are included in the examinations in Divinity; and, on the other hand, there is every reason to hope that Cathedral bodies will be supported in any effort which they can make to guide the later work of candidates for the diaconate, and of the younger clergy generally.

The conditions are favourable to co-operation between these two great bodies to which the training of the Candidates for Holy Orders is properly committed; and I venture to think that we have hitherto suffered greatly from the want of it. There are many subjects included in the course of a young theological student with which the Universities can deal more thoroughly than the examining council of the Bishop. And the episcopal examination would gain immeasurably (I must believe) in efficiency and solemnity if it were less scholastic and of a narrower range. Our present method of training candidates for Holy Orders, if it can be called a method, is hasty and partial; it has very little fitness for inspiring men with the desire to pursue the inquiries on which they have entered: it offers no scope for testing the teaching power of the student himself: it gives no place for adequate probation, no opportunity for seasonable withdrawal from uncongenial work. It is dispersive, perfunctory, unsympathetic, unsuggestive, unpractical.

This is a long and grave indictment, but I think that those who have taken part in the examinations for Holy Orders will allow that it is essentially true. Many candidates, no doubt, are happily able to shape a course for themselves, and nearly all are full of zeal and devotion; but for the most part they are burdened with the contents of text-books, and embarrassed by the multiplicity of subjects with which they have to deal; they are destitute of a clear view of the mutual relations and absolute importance of the constituent parts of their science: they are uncertain as to the elementary principles of criticism, and unfurnished with a clue to guide them in later work. As a natural consequence, they are impatient to give up pursuits which they have not seen in vital connection with their pastoral charge. The priest ceases to be a student, and unconsciously leaves one great part of his office unfulfilled. It is of course impossible to point out in detail how all these evils might (as far as I can be judge) be removed or lessened; how a series of graduated examinations might take the place of the present duplicate or triplicate examinations; how an ordinary student at Cambridge (for example) might be made to feel that from his first admission to the University he had entered on a definite course of instruction, leading up in order by succession to the subjects reserved for candidates for the Priesthood; how catechetical lectures on an extended scale might test and impress the results of reading; how such a method might naturally kindle something of professional enthusiasm, while it would preserve large and varied sympathies. And there is nothing unattainable, nothing even difficult of attainment in all this. But not to enter upon these wider questions, I will only select two topics as to which more might be done for candidates for Holy Orders, with a view to their public ministrations as teachers, than is yet done—(i) The exposition of Holy Scripture; and (ii) The use of Church History.

i. Considerably more than half of our Morning and Evening Prayer is taken up with passages from Holy Scripture, Canticles, Psalms, Lessons. There is no one of us, I suppose, who has not felt the richness of the mine thus opened to him, and who has not also felt its darkness. We are constrained, as it were, to heap up around us the precious ore, but we are not trained habitually to prepare it for use. How few of us clergymen understand the Psalter. How few of us can attach any real meaning to large sections of the Prophets. And for the people the reading must often be like the recitation of a charm, in an unknown tongue, instead of a stirring of the spiritual consciousness by the voice of God speaking through clear lessons of the past. It is not, I think, easy to overrate the loss and the harm which is thus incurred. The minister cannot but feel that the Divine message which is committed to him day by day is only partially delivered, and the congregation fall insensibly into the practice of substituting isolated phrases which they can understand, for the fulness of the teaching of Scripture. We rejoice rightly in the appeal which is constantly made in our services to the open Bible, but we are content to forego some of the highest blessings which an open Bible can bring. Something more is wanted than the elaborate treatment of a text. We want to be guided to the continuous sense of chapters and books. And it is difficult to see how we can consistently condemn prayers in an unknown tongue, and continue readings which require and do not receive interpretation.

Yet the obvious remedy is in no way alien from the spirit of our services. Some injunctions issued by Queen Elizabeth to the Eastern Cathedrals prescribed that after the first lesson the minister should give an exposition openly in the Choir. I do not know whether the direction was ever obeyed; but the introduction of the New Lectionary may supply an occasion for the modified adoption of a usage which might be of inestimable good. In the meantime it is in our power to give greater definiteness and prominence to the study and practice of exegesis in the training of the Clergy.

In the regular course of reading at Cambridge, a candidate for the ordinary degree of B.A., through the Special Theological Examination, is required to master the contents of the Old Testament, and two Gospels, the Acts of the Apostles, and two Epistles in the original Greek. It is evident that by some little arrangement the preparation of these subjects might be made to secure a fair acquaintance with the chief facts in Biblical criticism, with the groupings and characteristics of the different books of the Bible, with the relation of Scripture to other cognate writings. And, what is of far greater importance, I believe that even an indifferent scholar could be led in the way to feel what precious results he can himself gain by the faithful and independent use of his own slender power.

And here it will be seen that some division in the vast subject of Scriptural study might be made with the greatest advantage. All that is included in the term "Introduction" naturally belongs to the work of the University, and the University could give a guarantee for an adequate acquaintance with this part of the field. If such a guarantee were accepted by the Bishop, the candidate for the Diaconate would be able to concentrate his attention on a thorough preparation of some one or two books, which would then supply him with large materials in a form ready for his future ministrations. And in most cases the young deacon might be encouraged to take for continuous exposition the subjects selected for his examination for the priesthood. It is obvious how much the candidate and the congregation would gain at once, if the serious labour of preparation were thus made to contribute directly to the fulfilment of ministerial work. And for the future the teacher would obtain that perception of the infinite depth of Holy Scripture, which he could not lose afterwards. The later instruction of the pastor, who would be a student also, would then remain Scriptural in the highest sense, as giving the rich variety of the Divine methods and counsels and not those fragments of them which happened to be most consonant with his own feelings or wants.

ii. I have placed the use of Church History as the second subject to which greater attention should be paid with a view to the more efficient ministrations of our clergy. If the Old Testament can only be understood rightly when it is regarded as a prophetic preparation for the Gospel wrought out in many parts and in many fashions: so also the progress of the Church is most truly the life of the Risen Christ, clouded, marred, half hidden it may be, but never interrupted or suspended. We have suffered indeed grievously by cancelling or trying to cancel the medieval period in our own spiritual descent. But the time has come when we can claim our whole inheritance and use it. In this respect the outline of our University course needs revision. The periods commonly selected for study among us—the first three centuries and the English Reformation—tend to confirm the disastrous error which I have just noticed. But the necessary modifications could be easily made. A fair acquaintance with the broad outlines of the history of the Church and a thorough knowledge of some episode in it, might be obtained in the preparation for the ordinary degree. The latter exercise is as essential as the former. The mastering of abstracts must be supplemented by the study of some original documents, and if one or more alternative lives were offered, the student might select that which was according to his natural bent. But in some way he must be brought into personal contact with the heroes of Christendom. A few pages of Eusebius or Socrates: a few letters of Grosseteste: a volume of Luther's Table Talk, help us to live in a past very different from that which our imagination creates for the second or the fourth or the thirteenth or the sixteenth centuries.

Here again the whole range to be covered might be conveniently distributed between the University and the Episcopal Examinations. Without entering into details, I may say that it appears to me that the treatment of the subject should grow more and more minute and special, so that in the immediate preparation for the diaconate and the priesthood the student should be brought into the closest possible connection with the spiritual life of some great saint, from which he might draw inspiration and guidance for himself.

But however the subject is dealt with, I cannot but insist upon the need of making it vital and practical. If the exposition of Scripture is a necessary part of the work of the Christian teacher, I do not think that the exposition of Church History is in the present crisis less necessary. It is required alike by laity and clergy. Some of our most dangerous errors, some of our most depressing doubts would be removed if we could learn to look on earlier seasons of conflict and trial through the eyes of those who witnessed them. We should be less inclined to waste our strength on anachronisms if we could see from the orderly growth of the Christian Body, through periods of bitter sorrow and reproof, that new works are prepared for us to do which demand all our energies. We should be less inclined to distrust the future if we could see that God is no less present with us by His Spirit now than He has been with His Church always.

But if the minister is to use these studies, as we assume, for the instruction of his people, he must cultivate the power of speaking. The exposition and the sketch must be given freely, with every facility for developing, retouching, illustrating, repeating, according to the effect at the moment. How this power is to be cultivated, how the exercises by which it is to be tried can be made real, how they can be invested with interest, I do not venture to say. This work belongs rather to the pastoral training of the Cathedral than to the intellectual training of the University. Yet even here it is possible that the old institution of Acts could be restored under new conditions. But, at least, if the object is once recognised, those who are qualified to suggest the true method of attaining it will not refuse their help.

So far I have spoken of some parts of the training of the clergy in which they might be made more efficient for their public ministrations, but I have said nothing as to the supply of clergy. Indeed I do not think that there is any fear that the number of fit men ready to devote their lives to clerical work will fall short if the work be presented in its full range and dignity. If the supply be interrupted it will be because the duties of the office are not fairly set forth. It cannot but be that a ministry will always attract as many labourers as it can occupy, which is shown to offer scope for the freest exercise of thought, for the widest power of organisation, for the tenderest services of love, not for one kind of endowment only but for all. The higher the standard is fixed, the larger the claims that are made, the ampler the variety of gifts which is required, the more ready will men be to offer to Christ powers of mind and experience and affection.

For, however much it may be urged that the scheme of training which I have had in view is too ambitious for ordinary candidates in holy orders, I cannot admit for an instant the force of the objection. We get little because we ask little; and we shall get whatever we ask, knowing in Whose Name and for Whom we ask it.

But there is yet one point in this connection on which I wish to add a few words. I have said that I do not think that the supply of our regular clergy will fail, unless we hamper and misrepresent their work; but I do not think that they can ever give, or ever ought to give, all the spiritual instruction which the congregation requires. We must make vigorous endeavours to supplement our regular clergy by organized volunteers. Already a beginning has been made in this diocese by the appointment of readers; but the order must be increased and widened if we wish to reach the population of towns. And in saying this I do not contemplate a body of men who shall give up their whole time to visiting or teaching, but those rather who will undertake to do, with proper authority, some small yet definite work without abandoning their proper calling. It is, I believe, in this direction that we need most to seek recruits for a larger Christian ministry. There is abundant authority for such an institution in antiquity. There is abundant proof of its efficiency in the experience of modern Christian societies. We want deaconesses, and class-leaders, and lay-preachers on a large scale. We have not at present gained the active sympathy of the artisans or smaller tradesmen, in part because we have not used their due co-operation in our work. Still there are manifold offices which they can discharge, and they, better than any; and our conferences can fulfil no more useful function than that of calling out and organizing the offers of lay assistance in spiritual offices.

Just as theology takes up into itself all knowledge, and grows with the advance of the sciences, which it crowns by its peculiar truths, so the Christian ministry claims the recognised services of every part of the body, which, in turn, are consecrated by the divine commission of those who are set apart for it. The ideal of this catholicity of teaching, of this catholicity of service, is most noble, and I do not see that the attainment of it is in any way beyond hope.

VI.

THE ACTUAL STATE OF THINGS AT CAMBRIDGE.

*Read at the Church Congress at Leeds,
Oct. 10, 1872.*

VI.

THE ACTUAL STATE OF THINGS AT CAMBRIDGE.

It is natural that all who are interested in religious education should look at present with some anxiety to the future of our ancient Universities. Important changes in the character and course of the studies for which the great academic prizes are offered, have almost coincided in time with the general removal of the dogmatic restrictions which were formerly laid upon those who sought them. The anxiety is natural, and it is not groundless. There can be no doubt that the widening of the range of reading, and the abolition of tests in the Universities, have imposed new conditions of labour upon those of us to whom specific religious teaching within them is committed. We cannot realize these conditions too soon; and if I shall endeavour to shew that the actual circumstances in which we are placed open to us fresh opportunities for apprehending the fulness of our charge, and fresh motives for fulfilling it, I shall do so, not because I underrate the magnitude of the crisis, but for the very reason that I believe that we are now brought to the real trial of our faith. I shall do so, because I feel that the truth which we have to interpret must, if interpreted rightly, combine, co-ordinate, harmonize all the varied elements of human thought and knowledge; and that, therefore, it is beneficent necessity which constrains us to take a wider range in our survey of the facts of life: because I feel, when I look back upon the history of religious progress, that it may be through such intellectual and social movements as have at least reached us, that we shall best learn the lessons which GOD in His Providence is waiting to teach our generation: because, in a word, I feel that we are thus placed face to face with some of the greatest problems of the time, under circumstances which give a hope at least of their partial solution. This hope it is which I desire to bring prominently forward. And that it may have a substantial basis, we must be careful not to exaggerate the nature of the changes which have been made in the Universities. Regret is apt to make us blind; and the keen sense of what is lost dulls the power of seeing what remains. It has certainly been so with those who speak of the Universities as secularised. The fact is that henceforward the Universities and colleges present a two-fold character. So far as they are regarded in their individual members, they have no standard of opinion; but as societies they retain exactly the same religious character as they have had since the Reformation. Difficulties may perhaps arise hereafter in adjusting the claims of the individual with the claims of the society, but it is needless to dwell on these by anticipation. Experience has shown in other cases that a distinct religious character in the body can be reconciled with complete personal liberty. This then is the position which we have to make good. The changes in the constitution of the Universities might have been such as to render efficient religious action through their organisation impossible. If their religious character had been taken away from them; if restrictions had been imposed upon the freedom of religious teaching within their limits; if the prescribed religious teaching had been colourless, then I can well believe that those to whom the faith is justly more precious than all treasures besides, might have regarded them rather as fields, so to speak, of missionary enterprise than as societies through which they could work. But as it is, the Act which abolishes religious tests distinctly recognises and ratifies all that is essential to the true religious character of the Universities. The old epithets, hallowed by the memories of a thousand years, are solemnly rehearsed. Regular religious services are confirmed as a necessary part of the corporate life of all existing colleges. Provision is made that adequate religious instruction shall be furnished in them for students who belong to the Established Church. Offices which were restricted to persons in holy orders remain, so far as this Act is concerned, restricted as before. Special dogmatic tests are retained for those graduates who desire to enter the theological faculty. The preamble of the Act describes its scope as being the extension of the benefits "of the Universities... (and of the colleges and halls now subsisting therein) as places of religion and learning" to the whole nation..."under proper safeguard for the maintenance of religious instruction and worship."... It is said, I know, that these reservations to which we point are temporary and provisional; that in a few years whatever yet remains to connect the national Church with the Universities will be swept away; that worship will cease to be a common act; that dogmatic instruction will become obsolete; that clerical fellowships will be abolished; that theology will sink into the position of a purely literary pursuit. I can only reply that I see no ground for such anticipations in the existent state of feeling at Cambridge. But there are prophecies which have a fatal tendency to fulfil themselves; and if churchmen now act as if their fears were realised; if they isolate themselves; if they make no demands upon college teaching; if they shrink from reinforcing the ranks of the theological faculty; it is hard to see on what plea provisions can be retained which will become practically useless. For the present we have all that we require for successful activity; and successful activity will justify the position which we still hold. This being so, we are in no way concerned with the spirit in which some advocates of the late Act pressed its adoption and interpret its scope. Nor, on the other hand, do we dwell despondingly upon lost opportunities, which were, most unhappily, in a great measure unused, and therefore lost. We loyally accept the legislation which regulates the mode of our future action. We confidently trust to the enactments which preserve inviolate the religious character of our society as a whole. If we recall the greater privileges which have been swept away, it is that we may profit by the sibylline warning, and show that we rightly value, and desire to rightly use, those which are as yet assured to us.

This necessity will be forced upon us both by nobler obligations, and by the simple fact that we shall henceforth do our work more and more in the immediate presence of the most accomplished Nonconformist scholars. Perhaps we have needed the incentive; and it is not hard to see how the addition of a fresh body of students, who will naturally be for the most part laborious, grave, and simple in their habits, will be of the highest service to the Universities. This fresh element may in some degree counteract the growing luxury of our life, and bring back into due prominence the idea, which we have well-nigh lost, that the Universities are not clubs for the rich and indolent, but, above all things, places for devout self-denial and labour. In this respect we have much to learn from the social organisation of some of the isolated Christian societies around us; and if the lessons are brought before us in the equal and candid intercourse of university life, there is good promise that they will be under such circumstances most happily mastered and appropriated. The season is, no doubt, one of trial, but the conditions of the trial are not likely to grow more favourable if we shrink from adapting ourselves to them. We must use what we wish to keep exactly in proportion as we value our vantage-ground: we must employ it in the service of our faith. If it be lost, the responsibility of the loss rests with us. In the meantime, there is not, as far as my own experience goes, the least reason why, in consequence of recent changes, the atmosphere of the Universities should be less spiritual than it has been; why the beliefs which they gender and shape should be less firm or less distinct; why the life which they fashion and present should be less religious; but there is great reason why the ministers of Christ who find their work in them should fulfil their part with unwearied patience and with unfailing faith; there is great reason why all who love them, love them for the services they have rendered for long ages to GOD and to His truth, should encourage and inspire those who wish to preserve their ancient character by confidence and sympathy. Let it not be forgotten that the distrust of those to whom we look for help will paralyse even the strivings of faith.

It follows from what has been said that recent legislation need not prejudice the character of the Universities as places of religious education in the widest sense, if only those who duly value religious education loyally and hopefully use what they still have. But our thoughts here are necessarily turned with chief interest to the particular office which the Universities have hitherto discharged as training places of candidates for holy orders. Is there, then, any ground for fearing that they will hereafter be less fitted for this work than they have been? Must we, with however great sorrow, look forward to the time when the future clergy of our Church will no longer find in the studies which we pursue, in the discipline which we enforce, the true preparation for their ministry? I cannot, of course, venture to answer such questions, except so far as my own personal knowledge furnishes me with a reply; but when I compare the Cambridge of to-day with the Cambridge of five-and-twenty years ago, I do not scruple to say that the young theological student will find greater intellectual and spiritual advantages now than then; that he will find more efficient help, more personal sympathy, more watchful guidance.

But we must not in this respect unduly extend the office of the University. We must not be eager to anticipate there what belongs to a later period of ministerial preparation. That which the candidate for holy orders ought to look for at the University is intellectual training. His pastoral training belongs to another sphere. But it is of the gravest moment for his spiritual work what his intellectual training is. It must, to be worthy of the name, be such as to furnish him with a solid foundation for his special studies: it must be such as to place him in vital and intelligent connection, not only with the past but with the present: it must be such as to encourage him in every detail to look for truth and to welcome it from every quarter: it must be such as to expand and deepen the healthy energy and power of his higher life.

It is, perhaps, most difficult to judge dispassionately of that in which our own affections are centered; but I do believe that the candidate for holy orders will find these requirements satisfied among us. I will not repeat remarks which I made on a former occasion as to what appear to me to be the necessary foundations of all theological science, the free, devout, untiring study of Holy Scripture and of history. These studies the Universities have rightly placed in the forefront of their theological course. They can never be exhausted: they can never be barren. Again and again the young scholar will return to them as to a resting-place for faith, which experience will only make more firm and more fruitful.

At the same time, the Universities place the candidates for holy orders in a living relationship with the whole present world of thought. Let me endeavour to explain my meaning as briefly as I can. The peculiar difficulties which beset faith now seem to spring from two sources —from supposed consequences of the study of physics, and from supposed consequences of the study of life. It is argued, on the one hand, to put the case in the broadest light, that we are placed under a system of inevitable sequences; and, on the other, that the forms of religious belief are functions, so to speak, of particular stages of human progress, individual or national. The problems which arrange themselves under these two heads are unquestionably grave and urgent. They are problems which Christian students alone, as I believe, can solve, so far as it is given to man as yet to solve them; and they are problems which all Christian students who desire to see far into the depths of the Gospel ought to face.

For it is the especial glory of the Gospel that it deals, and deals necessarily, not only with the individual but also with the society, with the race, with the world. The great conceptions of the solidarity of life and the continuity of life are not simply independent productions of modern speculation; they are plainly written in the words of St. Paul and St. John; they are inherent in the facts of the Gospel history. Later discoveries, wider generalisations, larger experience, have at length illuminated these old truths; and so the Christian teachers of the coming generation are called with a Divine voice, which cannot be mistaken, to bring their message to bear upon the social questions which rise out of them. They are called, in other words, to exercise again the privilege of a spiritual power in concentrating, guiding, fulfilling the latest desires and aspirations of men.

If this be so, the very conflict of opinions, the very rivalry of studies, the very boldness and enthusiasm which belong to our actual University life, will, by God's blessing, minister to the growth and armament of faith. Neither in morals nor theology is ignorance the surest safeguard of lasting purity. Faith (our Christian faith) can, I am sure, use the conscious or unconscious services of every labourer for truth. It can claim and consecrate tribute from every region of the universe. It can move inviolate through every element and leave a blessing behind it. Faith is blanched and impoverished not in light but in darkness. It gains strength in the air and sunshine. Then it is crippled, dishonoured, imperilled, when it is isolated, when its supremacy is circumscribed, when its fresh springs of knowledge are stopped up. The true divine must be in sympathy with every science: the true son of faith is emphatically a son of light. I cannot, then, but believe that it is an inestimable advantage for students of theology that they should accomplish the first stages of their work in the closest intercourse with those who are engaged in other fields of labour, and guided by other methods of inquiry. By so doing, and hardly in any other way, will they become intelligently conversant with the adverse forces which they have to meet: they will find scattered treasures, which fall under their own domain. There may be some shipwrecks of faith in this mental commerce: the great deeps of thought cannot, in our imperfect state, be traversed without peril; but, on the whole, faith will grow stronger, and the interpretation of faith will grow wider and richer as the manifold relations of Christianity with every fragment of life become more clearly seen. And this wider vision cannot but be best gained in the Universities, where every form of intellectual activity ought to be freshest and most energetic. In saying this, I do not wish to deny that some dangerous tendencies have spread rapidly in the Universities as elsewhere during the last few years. I do not wish to deny that there is much restlessness and impatience in speculation: that there is some thoughtful and some superficial scepticism at Cambridge; but these tendencies are not the special product of the Universities, though they first reveal themselves there. They belong to a peculiar crisis in human progress, to a peculiar phase of society, to a peculiar stage in individual development. No seminary walls can exclude their influence. Sooner or later, our clergy will have to contend with them; and it is better that they should be first met when they can be calmly interrogated than that they should come as a surprise, when their opponents will be forced into a position of blind antagonism. There is, then, I venture to repeat, nothing in the constitution of University society, nothing in the freedom and width of University studies as they are now organised, which is necessarily antagonistic to the healthy development of religious life, nothing which may not be made to conduce to the right disciplining of a Christian minister. This freedom and breadth will furnish our candidates for holy orders with abundant occasions for self-control, for patience, for effort; but not without the promise of victory. They will impose upon our teachers the duty of unwearied watchfulness and care, of open-eyed and open-hearted sympathy, of strong and tender love, but not without the promise of a rich harvest. For the present we must be content with the promise.

It is premature to speak as yet of the results of the system of introductory reading which has been laid down for the new Theological Tripos at Cambridge; but it is not too much to believe that the close and thorough study of Holy Scripture, the familiar acquaintance with original records of Christian life and thought, the investigation of the gradual determination of doctrine which it enjoins, may be so guided as to prepare men to fulfil what I have indicated as the immediate work of our English Church: men who will hold fast all that they have received as the condition of fresh acquisitions: men who will know that growth is the sure sign of the vitality of faith: men who will have learnt by living experience that the Holy Spirit does not speak only at one time or in one way: men who will have the courage to assert and the wisdom to show that the Christian revelation reaches to and transfigures all that lies open to man in action or thought. These great hopes may not be fulfilled; but at least they are neither far-fetched nor unreasonable: they give strength for work which is often discouraging and always difficult: they carry with them, while they are still warm, some power of accomplishment: they fairly ask for support from all who remember with gratitude what they gained at the Universities of lofty and generous feeling, of wise and candid conviction; from all who have learnt by experience what the Universities can hereafter do for those who shall carry on with richer success what they have been able to begin for the Church of England and for the Church Catholic. It is quite possible that the view which I have endeavoured to give of the prospects of religious education at Cambridge may appear to some to be too bright; but I can only set down the impressions which I have myself received during the last two years. In the course of that time I have seen a large body of the younger men among us, including many of the highest University distinctions, unite themselves in a society upon the basis of communion with the Church of England, with the twofold object, to quote their own words, of "increasing the number of devoted and duly prepared workers in the cause of Christ, both clerical and lay, who go forth from the University," and "of promoting unity within the Church of England, to the extent of their opportunities[1]." I have seen the college tutors heartily and unanimously combine to provide efficient public instruction in the subjects proposed for the Theological Tripos, while two colleges (Trinity and Emmanuel) have appointed distinguished scholars without their own bodies to Theological Prælectorships. I have seen residents of the highest standing and of the most varied shades of opinion generously support the endeavour to give a substantive

---

[1] The Cambridge University Church Society. The words are quoted from a paper by "One of the Promoters." In the rules of the society its objects are described as being "to foster a deep and earnest resolve to devote time and energy in after life to Christian study and Christian work; to gain clearer views as to what are the special needs of the age, and as to the manner in which Christ's Gospel may be employed to supply them; to promote mutual charity and a sense of unity of purpose among all who have really at heart the furtherance of Christ's kingdom upon earth." The condition of membership is a written declaration that those who seek it are "regular communicants in the Church of England."

reality to Theological degrees, and to facilitate common action on the part of the members of the Theological Faculty. It is then impossible not to set these facts against the causes for anxiety which I do not attempt to dissemble. And there is this important difference between them. The causes for anxiety spring rather from the general tone of modern thought than from anything characteristic of the Universities themselves as they are now constituted: our encouragements, on the other hand, are due to the personal feelings of those with whom we have to work. But even if the circumstances under which we are called to act were far less favourable, it would still be our clear duty to recognise the Universities as the highest seats of religious education, till they abjure the title, and to work in the sure belief that they may, by God's help, be made to fulfil this, their noblest function, more and more perfectly. It would be a disastrous day for England, and for Christendom, if the candidates for the ministry of our Church were withdrawn in any large numbers from the chastening influences of wide and liberal discipline in a society as free and varied as that in which they will be called to exercise their ministry. No one can feel more deeply than I do the infinite importance of cultivating the spiritual life: no one can prize more highly the deposit of Christian doctrine which has been committed to our keeping; but I believe that our gravest religious dangers at the present time proceed, not from any prospective decay of personal devotion, not from any abandonment of the old landmarks of faith, but from the want of knowledge and the want of wisdom. We cannot shut our eyes to the speculative and social questions which day by day call more urgently for solution. We cannot doubt that a body which claims to be a spiritual power, and not merely a hierarchical caste, must accept the responsibility of meeting them. And they must be met not with answers which were shaped to meet other conditions, but with "new things" from the treasury of God. They must be dealt with not simply from without, but on the basis of intelligent sympathy, as phenomena of that vaster social life in which we all share and by which we are all moved. They present, in a word, the field on which we can accept, in the name and in the strength of our faith, the challenge which is thrown down to us on many sides, and show that the facts of the Incarnation, the Passion, the Resurrection of Christ, contain that which will meet the wants of the latest age. This is our peculiar work as Christian teachers, and the work of those who come after us. That we and they may grow familiar with its requirements, and be prepared to fulfil them, the ancient and religious Universities—it is a joy to repeat words so full of promise—offer us all their resources, the stern methods of physical science, the precise and delicate refinements of philology, the broad lessons of history and philosophy, the priceless opportunity of free and unselfish intercourse We cannot dispense with any one of these instruments of training in the study of theology; for theology is the science of all life, of all being.

We cannot reproduce them at our will under conditions equally favourable to their action. We cannot elsewhere than in the Universities learn the lessons which society has to teach us; we cannot elsewhere convey to society the lessons which we have to teach, as they may be learnt and taught, in the natural, unconstrained fellowship of a common life. We believe that our faith can assimilate every fragment of truth: let us openly show that we believe.

March 1873.

A CATALOGUE of THEOLOGICAL BOOKS, with a Short Account of their Character and Aim,

Published by

MACMILLAN AND CO.

Bedford Street, Covent Garden, London.

Abbott (Rev. E. A.)—Works by the Rev. E. A. ABBOTT, M.A., Head Master of the City of London School.

BIBLE LESSONS. Second Edition. Crown 8vo. 4s. 6d.

"*Wise, suggestive, and really profound initiation into religious thought.*"—Guardian. *The Bishop of St. David's, in his speech at the Education Conference at Abergwilly, says he thinks* "*nobody could read them without being the better for them himself, and being also able to see how this difficult duty of imparting a sound religious education may be effected.*"

THE GOOD VOICES: A Child's Guide to the Bible. With upwards of 50 Illustrations. Crown 8vo. cloth gilt. 5s.

"*It would not be easy to combine simplicity with fulness and depth of meaning more successfully than Mr. Abbott has done.*"—Spectator. *The* Times *says*—"*Mr. Abbott writes with clearness, simplicity, and the deepest religious feeling.*"

Ainger (Rev. Alfred).—SERMONS PREACHED IN THE TEMPLE CHURCH. By the Rev. ALFRED AINGER, M.A. of Trinity Hall, Cambridge, Reader at the Temple Church. Extra fcap. 8vo. 6s.

This volume contains twenty-four Sermons preached at various times during the last few years in the Temple Church, and are characterised by such qualities as are likely to make them acceptable to cultivated and thoughtful readers. The following are a few of the topics treated of:—"Boldness;" "Murder, Ancient and Modern;" "The Atonement;" "The Resurrection;" "The Fear of Death;" "The Forgiveness of Sins, the Remission of a Debt" (2 Sermons); "Anger, Noble and Ignoble;" "Culture and Temptation;" "The Religious Aspect of Wit and Humour;" "The Life of the Ascended Christ." "It is," the British Quarterly says, "the fresh unconventional talk of a clear independent thinker, addressed to a congregation of thinkers.... Thoughtful men will be greatly charmed by this little volume."

Alexander.—THE LEADING IDEAS of the GOSPELS. Five Sermons preached before the University of Oxford in 1870—71. By WILLIAM ALEXANDER, D.D., Brasenose College; Lord Bishop of Derry and Raphao; Select Preacher. Cr. 8vo. 4s. 6d.

Each of these Sermons is on a characteristic text taken successively from each of the four Gospels, there being two on that from St. John; viz.—St. Matt. i. 1; St. Mark i. 1; St. Luke i. 3; St. John i. 1, 14. "Dr. Alexander is eminently fitted for the task he has undertaken. He has a singular felicity of style, which lights up the discourse and clothes it with great beauty and impressiveness." —Nonconformist.

Arnold.—A BIBLE READING BOOK FOR SCHOOLS. THE GREAT PROPHECY OF ISRAEL'S RESTORATION (Isaiah, Chapters 40—66). Arranged and Edited for Young Learners. By MATTHEW ARNOLD, D.C.L., formerly Professor of Poetry in the University of Oxford, and Fellow of Oriel. Third Edition. 18mo. cloth. 1s.

Mr. Arnold has undertaken this really important task, on account of his conviction "of the immense importance in education of what is called letters; of the side which engages our feelings and imagination." In this little volume he attempts to do for the Bible what has been so abundantly done for Greek and Roman, as well as English authors; viz.—to take "some whole, of admirable literary beauty in style and treatment, of manageable length, within defined limits; and present this to the learner in an intelligible shape, adding such explanations and helps as may enable him to grasp it as a connected and complete work." The Times *says—" Whatever may be the fate of this little book in Government Schools, there can be no doubt that it will be found excellently calculated to further instruction in Biblical literature in any school into which it may be introduced... We can safely say that whatever school uses this book, it will enable its pupils to understand Isaiah, a great advantage compared with other establishments which do not avail themselves of it."*

Baring-Gould.—LEGENDS OF OLD TESTAMENT CHARACTERS, from the Talmud and other sources. By the Rev. S. BARING-GOULD, M.A., Author of "Curious Myths of the Middle Ages," "The Origin and Development of Religious Belief," "In Exitu Israel," etc. In two vols. crown 8vo. 16s. Vol. I. Adam to Abraham. Vol. II. Melchizidek to Zechariah.

Mr. Baring-Gould's previous contributions to the History of Mythology, and the formation of a science of comparative religion are admitted to be of the highest importance; the present work, it is believed, will be found of equal value. He has collected from the Talmud and other sources, Jewish and Mahommedan, a large number of curious and interesting legends concerning the principal characters of the Old Testament, comparing these frequently with similar legends current among many of the peoples, savage and civilised, all over the world. "These volumes contain much that is strange, and to the ordinary English reader, very novel."— Daily News.

Barry, Alfred, D.D.—The ATONEMENT of CHRIST. Six Lectures delivered in Hereford Cathedral during Holy Week, 1871. By ALFRED BARRY, D.D., D.C.L., Canon of Worcester, Principal of King's College, London. Fcap. 8vo. 2s. 6d.

In writing these Sermons, it has been the object of Canon Barry to set forth the deep practical importance of the doctrinal truths of the Atonement. "The one truth," says the Preface, "which, beyond all others, I desire that these may suggest, is the inseparable unity which must exist between Christian doctrine, even in its more mysterious forms, and Christian morality or devotion. They are a slight contribution to the plea of that connection of Religion and Theology, which in our own time is so frequently and, as it seems to me, so unreasonably denied." The Guardian *calls them* "*striking and eloquent lectures.*"

Benham.—A COMPANION TO THE LECTIONARY, being a Commentary on the Proper Lessons for Sundays and Holidays. By the Rev. W. BENHAM, B.D., Vicar of Margate. Crown 8vo. 7s. 6d.

This work is the result of many years' study on the part of the author, who has sought for assistance from the works of the ablest modern divines. The author's object is to give the reader a clear understanding of the Lessons of the Church, which he does by means of general and special introductions, and critical and explanatory notes on all words and passages presenting the least difficulty.

Binney.—SERMONS PREACHED IN THE KING'S WEIGH HOUSE CHAPEL, 1829—69. By THOMAS BINNEY, D.D. New and Cheaper Edition. Extra fcap. 8vo. 4s. 6d.

In the earnestness and vigour which characterize the sermons in this volume the reader will find a clue to the vast influence exerted by Mr. Binney for forty years over a wide circle, particularly young men. In the concluding sermon, preached after the publication of the first edition, he reviews the period of his ministry as a whole, dwelling especially on its religious aspects. "Full of robust intelligence, of reverent but independent thinking on the most profound and holy themes, and of earnest practical purpose."—London Quarterly Review.

Bradby.—SERMONS PREACHED AT HAILEYBURY. By E. H. BRADBY, M.A., Master. 8vo. [*Immediately.*

Burgon.—A TREATISE on the PASTORAL OFFICE. Addressed chiefly to Candidates for Holy Orders, or to those who have recently undertaken the cure of souls. By the Rev. JOHN W. BURGON, M.A., Oxford. 8vo. 12s.

The object of this work is to expound the great ends to be accomplished by the Pastoral office, and to investigate the various means by which these ends may best be gained. Full directions are given as to preaching and sermon-writing, pastoral visitation, village education and catechising, and confirmation. Under the heading of "Pastoral Method" the author shows how each of the occasional offices of the Church may be most properly conducted, as well as how a clergyman's ordinary public ministrations may be performed with the greatest success. The best methods of parochial management are examined, and an effort is made to exhibit the various elements of the true pastoral spirit. "The spirit in which it approaches and solves practical questions is at once full of common sense and at the same time marked by a deep reverential piety and a largeness of charity which are truly admirable."—Spectator.

Butler (G.)—Works by the Rev. GEORGE BUTLER, M.A., Principal of Liverpool College:

FAMILY PRAYERS. Crown 8vo. 5s.

The prayers in this volume are all based on passages of Scripture—the morning prayers on Select Psalms, those for the evening on portions of the New Testament.

SERMONS PREACHED in CHELTENHAM COLLEGE CHAPEL. Crown 8vo. 7s. 6d.

These Sermons, twenty-nine in number, were delivered at intervals from the opening of Cheltenham College Chapel in 1858, *to the last Sunday of the year* 1861, *and contain references to the important events which occurred during that period—the Indian mutiny, the French campaign in Italy, the liberation of Sicily and Naples, the establishment of the kingdom of Italy, the American Civil War, and the deaths of many eminent men. "These sermons are plain, practical, and well adapted to the auditors..... We cordially recommend the volume as a model of pulpit style, and for individual and family reading."*—Weekly Review.

Butler (Rev. H. M.)—SERMONS PREACHED in the CHAPEL OF HARROW SCHOOL. By H. MONTAGU BUTLER, Head Master. Crown 8vo. 7s. 6d.

> *Whilst these Sermons were prepared to meet the wants of a special class, there is a constant reference in them to the great principles which underlie all Christian thought and action. They deal with such subjects as "Temptation," "Courage," "Duty without regard to consequences," "Success," "Devout Impulses," and "The Soul's need of God." "These sermons are adapted for every household. There is nothing more striking than the excellent good sense with which they are imbued."*—Spectator.

A SECOND SERIES. Crown 8vo. 7s. 6d.

> *"Excellent specimens of what sermons should be,—plain, direct, practical, pervaded by the true spirit of the Gospel, and holding up lofty aims before the minds of the young."*—Athenæum.

Butler (Rev. W. Archer).—Works by the Rev. WILLIAM ARCHER BUTLER, M.A., late Professor of Moral Philosophy in the University of Dublin:—

SERMONS, DOCTRINAL AND PRACTICAL. Edited, with a Memoir of the Author's Life, by THOMAS WOODWARD, Dean of Down. With Portrait. Eighth and Cheaper Edition, 8vo. 8s.

> *The following selections from the titles of the sermons will give a fair idea of the contents of the volume:—"The Mystery of the Holy Incarnation;" "The Daily Self-Denial of Christ;" "The Power of the Resurrection;" "Self-Delusion as to our Real State before God;" "The Faith of Man and the Faithfulness of God;" "The Wedding-Garment;" "Human Affections Raised, not Destroyed by the Gospel;" "The Rest of the People of God;" "The Divinity of our Priest, Prophet, and King;" "Church Education in Ireland" (two Sermons). The Introductory Memoir narrates in considerable detail and with much interest, the events of Butler's brief life; and contains a few specimens of his poetry, and a few extracts from his addresses and essays, including a long and eloquent passage on the Province and Duty of the Preacher.*

Butler (Rev. W. Archer.)—*continued.*

A SECOND SERIES OF SERMONS. Edited by J. A. JEREMIE, D.D., Dean of Lincoln. Sixth and Cheaper Edition. 8vo. 7s.

In this volume are contained other twenty-six of the late Professor Butler's Sermons, embracing a wide range of Christian topics, as will be seen by the following selection from the titles:—"*Christ the Source of all Blessings;*" "*The Hope of Glory and the Charities of Life;*" "*The Holy Trinity;*" "*The Sorrow that Exalts and Sanctifies;*" "*The Growth of the Divine Life;*" "*The Folly of Moral Cowardice;*" "*Strength and Mission of the Church;*" "*The Blessedness of Submission;*" "*Eternal Punishment.*" *The* North British Review *says,* "*Few sermons in our language exhibit the same rare combination of excellencies; imagery almost as rich as Taylor's; oratory as vigorous often as South's; judgment as sound as Barrow's; a style as attractive but more copious, original, and forcible than Atterbury's; piety as elevated as Howe's, and a fervour as intense at times as Baxter's. Mr. Butler's are the sermons of a true poet.*"

LETTERS ON ROMANISM, in reply to Dr. Newman's Essay on Development. Edited by the Dean of Down. Second Edition, revised by Archdeacon HARDWICK. 8vo. 10s. 6d.

These Letters contain an exhaustive criticism of Dr. Newman's famous "*Essay on the Development of Christian Doctrine.*" *An attempt is made to shew that the theory is opposed to the received doctrine of the Romish Church; that it is based on purely imaginary grounds, and necessarily carries with it consequences in the highest degree dangerous both to Christianity and to general truth. Whilst the work is mainly polemical in its character, it contains the exposition of many principles of far more than mere temporary interest.* "*A work which ought to be in the Library of every student of Divinity.*"—BP. ST. DAVID'S.

LECTURES ON ANCIENT PHILOSOPHY. See SCIENTIFIC CATALOGUE.

Cambridge Lent Sermons.—SERMONS preached during Lent, 1864, in Great St. Mary's Church, Cambridge. By the BISHOP OF OXFORD, Revs. H. P. LIDDON, T. L. CLAUGHTON, J. R. WOODFORD, Dr. GOULBURN, J. W. BURGON, T. T. CARTER, Dr. PUSEY, Dean HOOK, W. J. BUTLER, Dean GOODWIN. Crown 8vo. 7s. 6d.

Campbell.—Works by JOHN M'LEOD CAMPBELL:—

THE NATURE OF THE ATONEMENT AND ITS RELATION TO REMISSION OF SINS AND ETERNAL LIFE. Third Edition, with an Introduction and Notes. 8vo. 10s. 6d.

Three chapters of this work are devoted to the teaching of Luther on the subject of the Atonement, and to Calvinism, as taught by Dr. Owen and President Edwards, and as recently modified. The remainder is occupied with the different aspects of the Atonement as conceived by the author himself, the object being partly to meet the objections of honest inquirers, but mainly so to reveal the subject in its own light as to render self-evident its adaptation to the spiritual wants of man. Professor Rolleston, in quoting from this book in his address to the Biological Section of the British Association (Liverpool, September, 1870), speaks of it as "the great work of one of the first of living theologians." "Among the first theological treatises of this generation."—Guardian.

CHRIST THE BREAD OF LIFE. An Attempt to give a profitable direction to the present occupation of Thought with Romanism. Second Edition, greatly enlarged. Crown 8vo. 4s. 6d.

In this volume the Doctrines of the Infallibility of the Church and Transubstantiation are regarded as addressed to real inward needs of humanity, and an effort is made to disengage them from the truths whose place they usurp, and to exhibit these truths as adequate to meet human cravings. The aim is, first, to offer help to those who feel the attractions to Romanism too strong to be overcome by direct arguments addressed to sense and reason; and, second, to quicken interest in the Truth itself. "Deserves the most attentive study by all who interest themselves in the predominant religious controversy of the day."—Spectator.

Campbell (J. M'Leod.)—*continued.*

REMINISCENCES AND REFLECTIONS, referring to his Early Ministry in the Parish of Row, 1825—31. Edited with an Introductory Narrative by his eldest Son, DONALD CAMPBELL, M.A., Chaplain of King's College, London. Crown 8vo. 7s. 6d.

The late Dr. McLeod Campbell was acknowledged to be a man of exceptional gifts and earnestness, and his early life was connected with one of the most exciting, interesting, and important controversies that ever agitated the Church of Scotland. These 'Reminiscences and Reflections,' written during the last year of his life, were mainly intended to place on record thoughts which might prove helpful to others,—and no one was more qualified to give such help to those who are earnestly seeking spiritual truth and peace. The author, in this work, deals with questions of vital momont, in a way that but few are qualified to do.

Canterbury.—THE PRESENT POSITION OF THE CHURCH OF ENGLAND. Seven Addresses delivered to the Clergy and Churchwardens of his Diocese, as his Charge, at his Primary Visitation, 1872. By ARCHIBALD CAMPBELL, Archbishop of Canterbury. Third Edition. 8vo. cloth. 3s. 6d.

The subjects of these Addresses are, I. Lay Co-operation. II. Cathedral Reform. III. and IV. Ecclesiastical Judicature. V. Ecclesiastical Legislation. VI. Missionary Work of the Church. VII. The Church of England in its relation to the Rest of Christendom. There are besides, a number of statistical and illustrative appendices.

Cheyne.—Works by T. K. CHEYNE, M.A., Fellow of Balliol College, Oxford :—

THE BOOK OF ISAIAH CHRONOLOGICALLY ARRANGED. An Amended Version, with Historical and Critical Introductions and Explanatory Notes. Crown 8vo. 7s. 6d.

The object of this edition is to restore the probable meaning of Isaiah, so far as can be expressed in appropriate English. The basis of the version is the revised translation of 1611, *but alterations have been introduced wherever the true sense of the prophecies appeared to require it. The* Westminster Review *speaks of it as* "a piece of

Cheyne (T. K.)—*continued.*

    scholarly work, very carefully and considerately done." The Academy calls it "a successful attempt to extend a right understanding of this important Old Testament writing."

NOTES AND CRITICISMS on the HEBREW TEXT OF ISAIAH. Crown 8vo. 2s. 6d.

This work is offered as a slight contribution to a more scientific study of the Old Testament Scriptures. The author aims at completeness, independence, and originality, and constantly endeavours to keep philology distinct from exegesis, to explain the form without pronouncing on the matter. Saad Yah's Arabic Version in the Bodleian has been referred to, while Walton and Buxtorf have been carefully consulted. The philological works of German critics, especially Ewald and Delitsch, have been anxiously and repeatedly studied. The Academy *calls the work "a valuable contribution to the more scientific study of the Old Testament."*

Choice Notes on the Four Gospels, drawn from Old and New Sources. Crown 8vo. 4s. 6d. each Vol. (St. Matthew and St. Mark in one Vol. price 9s.).

These Notes are selected from the Rev. Prebendary Ford's Illustrations of the Four Gospels, the choice being chiefly confined to those of a more simple and practical character. The plan followed is to go over the Gospels verse by verse, and introduce the remarks, mostly meditative and practical, of one or more noted divines, on the verses selected for illustration.

Church.—SERMONS PREACHED BEFORE the UNIVERSITY OF OXFORD. By the very Rev. R. W. Church, M.A., Dean of St. Paul's. Second Edition. Crown 8vo. 4s. 6d.

Sermons on the relations between Christianity and the ideas and facts of modern civilized society. The subjects of the various discourses are:—" The Gifts of Civilization," " Christ's Words and Christian Society," " Christ's Example," and " Civilization and Religion." " Thoughtful and masterly... We regard these sermons as a landmark in religious thought. They help us to understand the latent strength of a Christianity that is assailed on all sides."— Spectator.

Clay.—THE POWER OF THE KEYS. Sermons preached in Coventry. By the Rev. W. L. CLAY, M.A. Fcap. 8vo. 3s. 6d.

In this work an attempt is made to shew in what sense, and to what extent, the power of the Keys can be exercised by the layman, the Church, and the priest respectively. The Church Review *says the sermons are "in many respects of unusual merit."*

Clergyman's Self-Examination concerning the APOSTLES' CREED. Extra fcap. 8vo. 1s. 6d.

"These Confessions have been written by a clergyman for his own use. They speak of his own unbelief. Possibly they may help some of his brethren, who wish to judge themselves that they may not be ashamed before the Judge of all the earth."

Collects of the Church of England. With a beautifully Coloured Floral Design to each Collect, and Illuminated Cover. Crown 8vo. 12s. Also kept in various styles of morocco.

The distinctive characteristic of this edition is the coloured floral design which accompanies each Collect, and which is generally emblematical of the character of the day or saint to which it is assigned; the flowers which have been selected are such as are likely to be in bloom on the day to which the Collect belongs. "Carefully, indeed livingly drawn and daintily coloured," says the Pall Mall Gazette. *The* Guardian *thinks it "a successful attempt to associate in a natural and unforced manner the flowers of our fields and gardens with the course of the Christian year."*

Cotton.—Works by the late GEORGE EDWARD LYNCH COTTON, D.D., Bishop of Calcutta :—

SERMONS PREACHED TO ENGLISH CONGREGATIONS IN INDIA. Crown 8vo. 7s. 6d.

These Sermons are selected from those which were preached between the years 1863 *and* 1866 *to English congregations under the varied circumstances of place and season which an Indian Bishop encounters. "The sermons are models of what sermons should be, not only on account of their practical teachings, but also with regard to the singular felicity with which they are adapted to times, places, and circumstances."*—Spectator.

Cotton (G. E. L.)--*continued.*

EXPOSITORY SERMONS ON THE EPISTLES FOR THE SUNDAYS OF THE CHRISTIAN YEAR. Two Vols. Crown 8vo. 15s.

These two volumes contain in all fifty-seven Sermons. They were all preached at various stations throughout India, and from the nature of the circumstances which called them forth, the varied subjects of which they treat are dealt with in such a manner as is likely to prove acceptable to Christians in general.

Cure.—THE SEVEN WORDS OF CHRIST ON THE CROSS. Sermons preached at St. George's, Bloomsbury. By the Rev. E. CAPEL CURE, M.A. Fcap. 8vo. 3s. 6d.

Of these Sermons the John Bull *says, "They are earnest and practical;" the* Nonconformist, *"The Sermons are beautiful, tender, and instructive;" and the* Spectator *calls them "A set of really good Sermons."*

Curteis.—DISSENT in its RELATION to the CHURCH OF ENGLAND. Eight Lectures preached before the University of Oxford, in the year 1871, on the foundation of the late Rev. John Bampton, M.A., Canon of Salisbury. By GEORGE HERBERT CURTEIS, M.A., late Fellow and Sub-Rector of Exeter College; Principal of the Lichfield Theological College, and Prebendary of Lichfield Cathedral; Rector of Turweston, Bucks. 8vo. 14s.

In these Bampton Lectures the Author has endeavoured to accomplish three things:—I. To shew those who are in despair at the present divided aspect of Christendom, that from the Apostles' time downwards there has never been an age of the Church without similar internal conflicts; that if well managed, these dissensions may be kept within bounds, and made to minister to the life and movement of the whole polity; but if ill-managed, they are always liable to become a wasting fever instead of a healthy warmth. II. To present materials by which Churchmen might be aided in forming an intelligent and candid judgment as to what precisely these dissenting denominations really are; what it is they do, and what they claim to teach; and why it is they are now combining to bring the Church of England, if possible, to the ground. III. To point out some few indications of the wonderful and every way deplorable misapprehensions which have clothed the Church of England to their eyes in colours absolutely foreign to her true character; have ascribed to her doctrines absolutely contrary to her meaning; and have interpreted her customs in a way repellant to the Christian Common-sense of her own people.

Davies.—Works by the Rev. J. LLEWELYN DAVIES, M.A., Rector of Christ Church, St. Marylebone, etc. :—

THE WORK OF CHRIST; or, the World Reconciled to God. With a Preface on the Atonement Controversy. Fcap. 8vo. 6s.

The reader will here find, amongst others, sermons on "The forgiveness of sins," "Christ dying for men," "Sacrifice," "The Example of Christ," "The Baptism of Christ," "The Temptation of Christ," "Love, Divine and Human," "Creation by the Word," "Holy Seasons," and "The Coming of the Son of Man." The Preface is devoted to shewing that certain popular theories of the Atonement are opposed to the moral sense of mankind, and are not imposed on Christians by statements either in the Old or New Testaments.

SERMONS on the MANIFESTATION OF THE SON OF GOD. With a Preface addressed to Laymen on the present Position of the Clergy of the Church of England; and an Appendix on the Testimony of Scripture and the Church as to the possibility of Pardon in the Future State. Fcap. 8vo. 6s. 6d.

The Preface to this work is mainly occupied with the distinction between the essential and non-essential elements of the Christian faith, proving that the central religious controversy of the day relates, not, as many suppose, to such questions as the Inspiration of Scripture, but to the profounder question, whether the Son of God actually has been manifested in the person of Jesus of Nazareth. The grounds on which the Christian bases his faith are also examined. In the Appendix the testimony of the Bible and the Anglican formularies as to the possibility of pardon in the future

Davies (Rev. J. Llewelyn)—*continued.*

state is investigated. *The sermons, of which the body of the work is composed, treat of the great principles revealed in the words and acts of Jesus. "This volume, both in its substance, prefix, and suffix, represents the noblest type of theology now preached in the English Church."*—Spectator.

BAPTISM, CONFIRMATION, AND THE LORD'S SUPPER, as Interpreted by their Outward Signs. Three Expository Addresses for Parochial use. Fcap. 8vo., limp cloth. 1s. 6d.

The method adapted in these addresses is to set forth the natural and historical meaning of the signs of the two Sacraments and of Confirmation, and thus to arrive at the spiritual realities which they symbolize. The work touches on all the principal elements of a Christian man's faith.

THE EPISTLES of ST. PAUL TO THE EPHESIANS, THE COLOSSIANS, and PHILEMON. With Introductions and Notes, and an Essay on the Traces of Foreign Elements in the Theology of these Epistles. 8vo. 7s. 6d.

The chief aim of the translations and notes in the present volume is simply to bring out as accurately as possible the apostle's meaning. The General Introduction, treats mainly of the time and circumstances in which Paul is believed to have written these Epistles. To each Epistle there is a special critical introduction.

MORALITY ACCORDING TO THE SACRAMENT OF THE LORD'S SUPPER. Crown 8vo. 3s. 6d.

These discourses were preached before the University of Cambridge. They form a continuous exposition, and are directed mainly against the two-fold danger which at present threatens the Church—the tendency, on the one hand, to regard Morality as independent of Religion, and, on the other, to ignore the fact that Religion finds its proper sphere and criterion in the moral life.

Davies (Rev. J. Llewelyn)—*continued*.

THE GOSPEL and MODERN LIFE. Sermons on some of the Difficulties of the Present Day, with a Preface on a Recent Phase of Deism. Extra fcap. 8vo. 6s.

> *The "recent phase of Deism" examined in the preface to this volume is that professed by the "Pall Mall Gazette"—that in the sphere of Religion there are one or two "probable suppositions," but nothing more. The writer starts with an assumption that mankind are under a Divine discipline, and in the light of this conviction passes under review the leading religious problems which perplex thoughtful minds of the present day. Amongst other subjects examined are—"Christ and Modern Knowledge," "Humanity and the Trinity," "Nature," "Religion," "Conscience," "Human Corruption," and "Human Holiness." "There is probably no writer in the Church fairer or more thoroughly worth listening to than Mr. Llewellyn Davies, and this book will do more than sustain his already high reputation."*—Globe.

De Teissier.—Works by G. F. DE TEISSIER, B.D.:—

VILLAGE SERMONS, FIRST SERIES. Crown 8vo. 9s.

> *This volume contains fifty-four short Sermons, embracing many subjects of practical importance to all Christians. The* Guardian *says they are "a little too scholarlike in style for a country village, but sound and practical."*

VILLAGE SERMONS, SECOND SERIES. Crown 8vo. 8s. 6d.

> *"This second volume of Parochial Sermons is given to the public in the humble hope that it may afford many seasonable thoughts for such as are Mourners in Zion." There are in all fifty-two Sermons embracing a wide variety of subjects connected with Christian faith and practice.*

THE HOUSE OF PRAYER; or, a Practical Exposition of the Order for Morning and Evening Prayer in the Church of England. 18mo. extra cloth. 4s. 6d.

> *"There is in these addresses to the Christian reader," says the Introduction, an attempt to set forth the devotional spirit of our Church*

in her daily forms of Morning and Evening Prayer, by shewing how all the parts of them may have a just bearing upon Christian practice, and so may have a deep influence upon the conduct of all our honest worshippers, under every possible relation and circumstance of life." "For a certain devout tenderness of feeling and religious earnestness of purpose, this little book of Mr. De Teissier's is really noteworthy; and it is a book which grows upon you very much when you read it."—Literary Churchman.

Ecce Homo. A SURVEY OF THE LIFE AND WORK OF JESUS CHRIST. 23rd Thousand. Crown 8vo. 6s.

"*A very original and remarkable book, full of striking thought and delicate perception; a book which has realised with wonderful vigour and freshness the historical magnitude of Christ's work, and which here and there gives us readings of the finest kind of the probable motive of His individual words and actions.*"—Spectator. "*The best and most established believer will find it adding some fresh buttresses to his faith.*"—Literary Churchman. "*If we have not misunderstood him, we have before us a writer who has a right to claim deference from those who think deepest and know most.*"—Guardian.

Faber.—SERMONS AT A NEW SCHOOL. By the Rev. ARTHUR FABER, M.A., Head Master of Malvern College. Cr. 8vo. [*Immediately.*

Farrar.—Works by the Rev. F. W. FARRAR, M.A., F.R.S., Head Master of Marlborough College, and Hon. Chaplain to the Queen :—

THE FALL OF MAN, AND OTHER SERMONS. Second and Cheaper Edition. Extra fcap. 8vo. 4s. 6d.

This volume contains twenty Sermons. No attempt is made in these sermons to develope a system of doctrine. In each discourse some one aspect of truth is taken up, the chief object being to point out its bearings on practical religious life. The Nonconformist says of these Sermons,—"*Mr. Farrar's Sermons are almost perfect specimens of one type of Sermons, which we may concisely call*

Farrar (Rev. F. W.)—*continued.*

beautiful. The style of expression is beautiful—there is beauty in the thoughts, the illustrations, the allusions—they are expressive of genuinely beautiful perceptions and feelings." The British Quarterly *says,—"Ability, eloquence, scholarship, and practical usefulness, are in these Sermons combined in a very unusual degree."*

THE WITNESS OF HISTORY TO CHRIST. Being the Hulsean Lectures for 1870. New Edition. Crown 8vo. 5s.

The copious notes contain many references which will be found of great use to the enquiring student. The following are the subjects of the Five Lectures:—I. "The Antecedent Credibility of the Miraculous." II. "The Adequacy of the Gospel Records." III. "The Victories of Christianity." IV. "Christianity and the Individual." V. "Christianity and the Race." The subjects of the four Appendices are:—A. "The Diversity of Christian Evidences." B. "Confucius." C. "Buddha." D. "Comte."

SEEKERS AFTER GOD. The Lives of Seneca, Epictetus, and Marcus Aurelius. *See* SUNDAY LIBRARY at end of Catalogue.

Fellowship: LETTERS ADDRESSED TO MY SISTER MOURNERS. Fcap. 8vo. cloth gilt. 3s. 6d.

"A beautiful little volume, written with genuine feeling, good taste, and a right appreciation of the teaching of Scripture relative to sorrow and suffering."—Nonconformist. *"A very touching, and at the same time a very sensible book. It breathes throughout the truest Christian spirit."*—Contemporary Review.

Forbes.—THE VOICE OF GOD IN THE PSALMS. By GRANVILLE FORBES, Rector of Broughton. Cr. 8vo. 6s. 6d.

This volume contains a connected series of twenty Sermons, divided into three parts, the two first parts being Introductory. Part I. treats of the "Ground of Faith," and consists of four Sermons on "Faith in God," "God's Voice within us," "Faith in God the Ground of Faith in the Bible," and "God's Voice in the Bible." Part II. treats of "The Voice of God in the Law and the Prophets," on which there are four Sermons; and Part III., occupying the greater part of the volume, deals with "The Voice of God in the Psalms," and consists of twelve Sermons. The last Sermon is on "The Voice of God in History."

Gifford.—THE GLORY OF GOD IN MAN. By E. H. GIFFORD, D.D. Fcap. 8vo., cloth. 3s. 6d.

"*The sermons are short, thoughtful, and earnest discussions of the weighty matter involved in the subjects of them.*"—Journal of Sacred Literature.

Golden Treasury Psalter. See p. 50.

Hardwick.—Works by the Ven. ARCHDEACON HARDWICK:

CHRIST AND OTHER MASTERS. A Historical Inquiry into some of the Chief Parallelisms and Contrasts between Christianity and the Religious Systems of the Ancient World. New Edition, revised, and a Prefatory Memoir by the Rev. FRANCIS PROCTER, M.A. Two vols. crown 8vo. 15s.

After several introductory chapters dealing with the religious tendencies of the present age, the unity of the human race, and the characteristics of Religion under the Old Testament, the Author proceeds to consider the Religions of India, China, America, Oceanica, Egypt, and Medo-Persia. The history and characteristics of these Religions are examined, and an effort is made to bring out the points of difference and affinity between them and Christianity. The object is to establish the perfect adaptation of the latter faith to human nature in all its phases and at all times. "*The plan of the work is boldly and almost nobly conceived... We commend the work to the perusal of all those who take interest in the study of ancient mythology, without losing their reverence for the supreme authority of the oracles of the living God.*"—Christian Observer.

A HISTORY OF THE CHRISTIAN CHURCH. Middle Age. From Gregory the Great to the Excommunication of Luther, Edited by WILLIAM STUBBS, M.A., Regius Professor of Modern History in the University of Oxford. With Four Maps constructed for this work by A. KEITH JOHNSTON. Third Edition. Crown 8vo. 10s. 6d.

Although the ground-plan of this treatise coincides in many points

Hardwick (Archd.)—*continued.*

with that of the colossal work of Schröckh, yet in arranging the materials a very different course has frequently been pursued. With regard to his opinions the late author avowed distinctly that he construed history with the specific prepossessions of an Englishman and a member of the English Church. The reader is constantly referred to the authorities, both original and critical, on which the statements are founded. For this edition Professor Stubbs has carefully revised both text and notes, making such corrections of facts, dates, and the like as the results of recent research warrant. The doctrinal, historical, and generally speculative views of the late author have been preserved intact. "As a Manual for the student of ecclesiastical history in the Middle Ages, we know no English work which can be compared to Mr. Hardwick's book."
—Guardian.

A HISTORY of the CHRISTIAN CHURCH DURING THE REFORMATION. New Edition, revised by Professor STUBBS. Crown 8vo. 10s. 6d.

This volume is intended as a sequel and companion to the "History of the Christian Church during the Middle Age." The author's earnest wish has been to give the reader a trustworthy version of those stirring incidents which mark the Reformation period, without relinquishing his former claim to characterise peculiar systems, persons, and events according to the shades and colours they assume, when contemplated from an English point of view, and by a member of the Church of England.

Hervey.—THE GENEALOGIES OF OUR LORD AND SAVIOUR JESUS CHRIST, as contained in the Gospels of St. Matthew and St. Luke, reconciled with each other, and shown to be in harmony with the true Chronology of the Times. By Lord ARTHUR HERVEY, Bishop of Bath and Wells. 8vo. 10s. 6d.

The difficulties and importance of the subject are first stated, the three main points of inquiry being clearly brought out. The Author then proceeds to shew that the genealogies of St. Matthew's and St. Luke's Gospels are both genealogies of Joseph, and examines the principle on which they are framed. In the following chapters the remaining aspects of the subject are exhaustively investigated.

Hymni Ecclesiæ.—Fcap. 8vo. 7s. 6d.

A selection of Latin Hymns of the Mediæval Church, containing selections from the Paris Breviary, and the Breviaries of Rome, Salisbury, and York. The selection is confined to such holy days and seasons as are recognised by the Church of England, and to special events or things recorded in Scripture. This collection was edited by Dr. Newman while he lived at Oxford.

Kempis, Thos. A.—DE IMITATIONE CHRISTI. LIBRI IV. Borders in the Ancient Style, after Holbein, Durer, and other Old Masters, containing Dances of Death, Acts of Mercy, Emblems, and a variety of curious ornamentations. In white cloth, extra gilt. 7s. 6d.

The original Latin text has been here faithfully reproduced. The Spectator *says of this edition, it "has many solid merits, and is perfect in its way." While the* Athenæum *says, "The whole work is admirable; some of the figure compositions have extraordinary merit."*

Kingsley.—Works by the Rev. CHARLES KINGSLEY, M.A., Rector of Eversley, and Canon of Chester. (For other Works by the same author, *see* HISTORICAL and BELLES LETTRES CATALOGUES).

The high merits of Mr. Kingsley's Sermons are acknowledged. Whether preached to the rustic audience of a village Church or to the princely congregation of the Chapel Royal, these Sermons are invariably characterized by intense earnestness and magnanimity, combined with genuine charity and winning tenderness; the style is always clear, simple, and unaffectedly natural, abounding in beautiful illustration, the fruit of a rich fancy and a cultivated taste. They are emphatically practical.

THE WATER OF LIFE, AND OTHER SERMONS. Second Edition. Fcap. 8vo. 3s. 6d.

This volume contains twenty-one Sermons preached at various places —Westminster Abbey, Chapel Royal, before the Queen at Windsor, etc. The following are a few of the titles:—"The Water of Life;" "The Wages of Sin;" "The Battle of Life;" "Ruth;" "Friend-

Kingsley (Rev. C.)—*continued.*

ship, or David and Jonathan;" "Progress;" "Faith;" "The Meteor Shower" (1866); *"Cholera"* (1866); *" The God of Nature."*

VILLAGE SERMONS. Seventh Edition. Fcap. 8vo. 3s. 6d.

The following are a few of the titles of these Sermons:—*"God's World;" "Religion not Godliness;" "Self-Destruction;" "Hell on Earth;" "Noah's Justice;" "Our Father in Heaven;" " The Transfiguration;" " The Crucifixion;" " The Resurrection;" "Improvement;" "On Books;" " The Courage of the Saviour."*

THE GOSPEL OF THE PENTATEUCH. Second Edition. Fcap. 8vo. 3s. 6d.

This volume consists of eighteen Sermons on passages taken from the Pentateuch. They are dedicated to Dean Stanley out of gratitude for his Lectures on the Jewish Church, *under the influence and in the spirit of which they were written. "With your book in my hand," Mr. Kingsley says in his Preface, " I have tried to write a few plain Sermons, telling plain people what they will find in the Pentateuch. I have told them that they will find in the Bible, and in no other ancient book, that living working God, whom their reason and conscience demand; and that they will find that He is none other than Jesus Christ our Lord."*

GOOD NEWS OF GOD. Fourth Edition. Fcap. 8vo. 3s. 6d.

This volume contains thirty-nine short Sermons, preached in the ordinary course of the author's parochial ministrations. A few of the titles are—*" The Beatific Vision;" " The Life of God;" "The Song of the Three Children;" "Worship;" "De Profundis;" " The Race of Life;" "Heroes and Heroines;" "Music;" "Christ's Boyhood;" "Human Nature;" " True Prudence;" " The Temper of Christ;" "Our Deserts;" " The Loftiness of God."*

SERMONS FOR THE TIMES. Third Edition. Fcap. 8vo. 3s. 6d.

Here are twenty-two Sermons, all bearing more or less on the every-

Kingsley (Rev. C.)—*continued.*

day life of the present day, including such subjects as these:—"Fathers and Children;" "A Good Conscience;" "Names;" "Sponsorship;" "Duty and Superstition;" "England's Strength;" "The Lord's Prayer;" "Shame;" "Forgiveness";" The True Gentleman;" "Public Spirit."

TOWN AND COUNTRY SERMONS. Second Edition. Extra fcap. 8vo. 3s. 6d.

Some of these Sermons were preached before the Queen, and some in the performance of the writer's ordinary parochial duty. There are thirty-nine in all, under such titles as the following:—"How to keep Passion-Week;" "A Soldier's Training;" "Turning-points;" "Work;" "The Rock of Ages;" "The Loftiness of Humility;" "The Central Sun;" "Εν Τουτω Νικα;" "The Eternal Manhood;" "Hypocrisy;" "The Wrath of Love." Of these Sermons the Nonconformist *says, "They are warm with the fervour of the preacher's own heart, and strong from the force of his own convictions. There is nowhere an attempt at display, and the clearness and simplicity of the style make them suitable for the youngest or most unintelligent of his hearers."*

SERMONS on NATIONAL SUBJECTS. Second Edition. Fcap. 8vo. 3s. 6d.

THE KING OF THE EARTH, and other Sermons, a Second Series of Sermons on National Subjects. Second Edition. Fcap. 8vo. 3s. 6d.

The following extract from the Preface to the 2nd Series will explain the preacher's aim in these Sermons:—" I have tried......to proclaim the Lord Jesus Christ, as the Scriptures, both in their strictest letter and in their general method, from Genesis to Revelation, seem to me to proclaim Him; not merely as the Saviour of a few elect souls, but as the light and life of every human being who enters into the world; as the source of all reason, strength, and virtue in heathen or in Christian; as the King and Ruler of

Kingsley (Rev. C.)—*continued.*

the whole universe, and of every nation, family, and man on earth; as the Redeemer of the whole earth and the whole human race...... His death, as a full, perfect, and sufficient sacrifice, oblation, and satisfaction for the sins of the whole world, by which God is reconciled to the whole human race.

DISCIPLINE, AND OTHER SERMONS. Fcp. 8vo. 3s. 6d.

Herein are twenty-four Sermons preached on various occasions, some of them of a public nature—at the Volunteer Camp, Wimbledon, before the Prince of Wales at Sandringham, at Wellington College, etc. A few of the titles are—"Discipline" (to Volunteers); "Prayer and Science;" "False Civilization;" "The End of Religion;" "The Humanity of God;" "God's World;" "Self-Help;" "Toleration;" "The Likeness of God." This volume the Nonconformist *calls,—"Eminently practical and appropriate ...... Earnest stirring words." The* Guardian *says,—"There is much thought, tenderness, and devoutness of spirit in these Sermons, and some of them are models both in matter and expression."*

DAVID. FOUR SERMONS: David's Weakness—David's Strength—David's Anger—David's Deserts. Fcap. 8vo. 2s. 6d.

These four Sermons were preached before the University of Cambridge, and are specially addressed to young men. Their titles are,—"David's Weakness;" "David's Strength;" "David's Anger;" "David's Deserts." The Freeman *says—"Every paragraph glows with manly energy, delivers straightforward practical truths, in a vigorous, sometimes even passionate way, and exhibits an intense sympathy with everything honest, pure, and noble."*

Lightfoot.—Works by J. B. LIGHTFOOT, D.D., Hulsean Professor of Divinity in the University of Cambridge; Canon of St. Paul's.

ST. PAUL'S EPISTLE TO THE GALATIANS. A Revised Text, with Introduction, Notes, and Dissertations. Third Edition, revised. 8vo. cloth. 12s.

The subjects treated in the Introduction are—the Galatian people, the

Lightfoot (Dr. J. B.)—*continued.*

Churches of Galatia, the date and genuineness of the Epistle, and its character and contents. The dissertations discuss the question whether the Galatians were Celts or Tartars, and the whole subject of " The Brethren of the Lord," and " St. Paul and the Three." While the Author's object has been to make this commentary generally complete, he has paid special attention to everything relating to St. Paul's personal history and his intercourse with the Apostles and Church of the Circumcision, as it is this feature in the Epistle to the Galatians which has given it an overwhelming interest in recent theological controversy. The Spectator says *"there is no commentator at once of sounder judgment and more liberal than Dr. Lightfoot."*

ST. PAUL'S EPISTLE TO THE PHILIPPIANS. A Revised Text, with Introduction, Notes, and Dissertations. Second Edition. 8vo. 12s.

The plan of this volume is the same as that of " The Epistle to the Galatians." The Introduction deals with the following subjects: —*" St. Paul in Rome," " Order of the Epistles of the Captivity," " The Church of Philippi," "Character and Contents of the Epistle,"' and its genuineness. The Dissertations are on " The Christian Ministry," " St. Paul and Seneca," and " The Letters of Paul and Seneca." "No commentary in the English language can be compared with it in regard to fulness of information, exact scholarship, and laboured attempts to settle everything about the epistle on a solid foundation."*—Athenæum. *" Its author blends large and varied learning with a style as bright and easy, as telling and artistic, as that of our most accomplished essayists."*—Nonconformist.

ST. CLEMENT OF ROME, THE TWO EPISTLES TO THE CORINTHIANS. A Revised Text, with Introduction and Notes. 8vo. 8s. 6d.

This volume is the first part of a complete edition of the Apostolic Fathers. The Introductions deal with the questions of the genuineness and authenticity of the Epistles, discuss their date and character,

Lightfoot (Dr. J. B.)—*continued.*

and analyse their contents. An account is also given of all the different epistles which bear the name of Clement of Rome. "By far the most copiously annotated edition of St. Clement which we yet possess, and the most convenient in every way for the English reader."—Guardian.

ON A FRESH REVISION OF THE ENGLISH NEW TESTAMENT. Second Edition. Crown 8vo. 6s.

The Author begins with a few words on S. Jerome's revision of the Latin Bible, and then goes on to shew in detail the necessity for a fresh revision of the authorized version on the following grounds:—1. False Readings. 2. Artificial distinctions created. 3. Real distinctions obliterated. 4. Faults of Grammar. 5. Faults of Lexicography. 6. Treatment of Proper Names, official titles, etc. 7. Archaisms, defects in the English, errors of the press, etc. The volume is completed by (1) an elaborate appendix on the words ἐπιούσιος and περιούσιος, (2) a table of passages of Scripture quoted, and (3) a general index. "The book is marked by careful scholarship, familiarity with the subject, sobriety, and circumspection."—Athenæum. "It abounds with evidence of the most extensive learning, and of a masterly familiarity with the best results of modern Greek scholarship."—Standard.

Luckock.—THE TABLES OF STONE. A Course of Sermons preached in All Saints' Church, Cambridge, by H. M. LUCKOCK, M.A., Vicar. Fcap. 8vo. 3s. 6d.

Sermons illustrative of the great principles of morality, mostly based on texts from the New Testament Scriptures.

Maclaren.—SERMONS PREACHED at MANCHESTER. By ALEXANDER MACLAREN. Third Edition. Fcap. 8vo. 4s. 6d.

These Sermons, twenty-four in number, are well known for the freshness and vigour of their thought, and the wealth of imagination they display. They represent no special school, but deal with the broad principles of Christian truth, especially in their bearing on

Maclaren (A.)—*continued.*

practical, every day life. A few of the titles are:—"*The Stone of Stumbling,*" "*Love and Forgiveness,*" "*The Living Dead,*" "*Memory in Another World,*" "*Faith in Christ,*" "*Love and Fear,*" "*The Choice of Wisdom,*" "*The Food of the World.*"

A SECOND SERIES OF SERMONS. Second Edition. Fcap. 8vo. 4s. 6d.

This 2nd Series, consisting of nineteen Sermons, are marked by the same characteristics as the 1st. *The* Spectator *characterises them as "vigorous in style, full of thought, rich in illustration, and in an unusual degree interesting."*

Maclear.—Works by G. F. MACLEAR, D.D., Head Master of King's College School :—

A CLASS-BOOK OF OLD TESTAMENT HISTORY. With Four Maps. Sixth Edition. 18mo. 4s. 6d.

"*The present volume,*" *says the Preface,* "*forms a Class-Book of Old Testament History from the Earliest Times to those of Ezra and Nehemiah. In its preparation the most recent authorities have been consulted, and wherever it has appeared useful, Notes have been subjoined illustrative of the Text, and, for the sake of more advanced students, references added to larger works. The Index has been so arranged as to form a concise Dictionary of the Persons and Places mentioned in the course of the Narrative." The Maps, prepared by Stanford, materially add to the value and usefulness of the book. The* British Quarterly Review *calls it "A careful and elaborate, though brief compendium of all that modern research has done for the illustration of the Old Testament. We know of no work which contains so much important information in so small a compass."*

A CLASS-BOOK OF NEW TESTAMENT HISTORY. Including the Connexion of the Old and New Testament. Fourth Edition. 18mo. 5s. 6d.

The present volume forms a sequel to the Author's Class-Book of Old Testament History, and continues the narrative to the close of

Maclear (G. F.)—*continued.*

St. Paul's second imprisonment at Rome. It is marked by the same characteristics as the former work, and it is hoped that it may prove at once a useful Class-Book and a convenient companion to the study of the Greek Testament. The work is divided into three Books—I. The Connection between the Old and New Testaments. II. The Gospel History. III. The Apostolic History. In the Appendix are given Chronological Tables The Clerical Journal *says, " It is not often that such an amount of useful and interesting matter on biblical subjects, is found in so convenient and small a compass, as in this well-arranged volume."*

A CLASS-BOOK OF THE CATECHISM OF THE CHURCH OF ENGLAND. Second Edition. 18mo. cloth. 2s. 6d.

The present work is intended as a sequel to the two preceding books. "Like them, it is furnished with notes and references to larger works, and it is hoped that it may be found, especially in the higher forms of our Public Schools, to supply a suitable manual of instruction in the chief doctrines of our Church, and a useful help in the preparation of Candidates for Confirmation." The Author goes over the Church Catechism clause by clause, and gives all needful explanation and illustration, doctrinal, practical, and historical; the Notes make the work especially valuable to the student and clergyman. Appended are a General Index, an Index of Greek and Latin Words, and an Index of the Words explained throughout the book. The Literary Churchman *says, "It is indeed the work of a scholar and divine, and as such, though extremely simple, it is also extremely instructive. There are few clergy who would not find it useful in preparing candidates for Confirmation; and there are not a few who would find it useful to themselves as well."*

A FIRST CLASS-BOOK OF THE CATECHISM OF THE CHURCH OF ENGLAND, with Scripture Proofs for Junior Classes and Schools. Second Edition. 18mo. 6d.

This is an epitome of the larger Class-book, meant for junior students and elementary classes. The book has been carefully condensed, so

Maclear (G. F.)—*continued.*

as to contain clearly and fully, the most important part of the contents of the larger book. Like it the present Manual is subdivided into five parts, each part into a number of short chapters, one or more of which might form a suitable lesson, and each chapter is subdivided in a number of sections, each with a prominent title indicative of its contents. It will be found a valuable Manual to all who are concerned with the religious training of children.

A SHILLING-BOOK of OLD TESTAMENT HISTORY.
18mo. cloth limp. 1s.

This Manual bears the same relation to the larger Old Testament History, that the book just mentioned does to the larger work on the Catechism. As in it, the small-type notes have been omitted, and a clear and full epitome given of the larger work. It consists of Ten Books, divided into short chapters, and subdivided into sections, each section treating of a single episode in the history, the title of which is given in bold type. The Map is clearly printed, and not overcrowded with names.

A SHILLING-BOOK of NEW TESTAMENT HISTORY.
18mo. cloth limp. 1s.

This bears the same relation to the larger New Testament History that the work just mentioned has to the large Old Testament History, and is marked by similar characteristics.

THE ORDER OF CONFIRMATION. A Sequel to the Class-Book of the Church Catechism, with Prayers and Collects. 18mo. 3d.

The Order of Confirmation is given in full, after which the Manual is divided into seven brief chapters:—I. "The Meaning of Confirmation." II. "The Origin of Confirmation." III., IV., V. "The Order of Confirmation," treating, (1) of "The Interrogation and Answer," (2) "The Laying on of Hands," (3) "The Prayers and Benediction," VI. "The Holy Communion." Chapter VII. consists of a few suitable Prayers and

Maclear (G. F.)—*continued.*

Collects intended to be used by the candidate during the days of preparation for Confirmation. The Literary Churchman *calls it "An admirable Manual. Thoroughly sound, clear, and complete in its teaching, with some good, clear, personal advice as to Holy Communion, and a good selection of prayers and collects for those preparing for Confirmation."*

Macmillan.—Works by the Rev. HUGH MACMILLAN. (For other Works by the same Author, see CATALOGUE OF TRAVELS and SCIENTIFIC CATALOGUE).

THE TRUE VINE; or, the Analogies of our Lord's Allegory. Second Edition. Globe 8vo. 6s.

This work is not merely an exposition of the fifteenth chapter of St. John's Gospel, but also a general parable of spiritual truth from the world of plants. It describes a few of the points in which the varied realm of vegetable life comes into contact with the higher spiritual realm, and shews how rich a field of promise lies before the analogical mind in this direction. The majority of the analogies are derived from the grape-vine; but the whole range of the vegetable kingdom is laid under contribution for appropriate illustration. Indeed, Mr. Macmillan has brought into his service many of the results of recent scientific and historic research and biblical criticism; as well as the discoveries of travellers ancient and modern. The work will thus be found not only admirably suited for devotional reading, but also full of valuable and varied instruction. The Nonconformist *says, "It abounds in exquisite bits of description, and in striking facts clearly stated."* The British Quarterly *says, "Readers and preachers who are unscientific will find many of his illustrations as valuable as they are beautiful."*

BIBLE TEACHINGS IN NATURE. Seventh Edition. Globe 8vo. 6s.

In this volume the author has endeavoured to shew that the teaching of nature and the teaching of the Bible are directed to the same great end; that the Bible contains the spiritual truths which are

Macmillan (H.)—*continued.*

necessary to make us wise unto salvation, and the objects and scenes of nature are the pictures by which these truths are illustrated. The first eight chapters describe, as it were, the exterior appearance of nature's temple—the gorgeous, many-coloured curtain hanging before the shrine. The last seven chapters bring us into the interior—the holy place, where is seen the very core of symbolical ordinances. "He has made the world more beautiful to us, and unsealed our ears to voices of praise and messages of love that might otherwise have been unheard."—British Quarterly Review. *"Mr. Macmillan has produced a book which may be fitly described as one of the happiest efforts for enlisting physical science in the direct service of religion."*—Guardian.

THE MINISTRY OF NATURE. Second Edition. Globe 8vo. 6s.

Mr. Macmillan believes that nature has a spiritual as well as a material side,—that she exists not only for the natural uses of the body, but also for the sustenance of the life of the soul. This higher ministry, the author believes, explains all the beauty and wonder of the world, which would often be superfluous or extravagant. In this volume of fourteen chapters the Author attempts to interpret Nature on her religious side in accordance with the most recent discoveries of physical science, and to shew how much greater significance is imparted to many passages of Scripture and many doctrines of Christianity when looked at in the light of these discoveries. Instead of regarding Physical Science as antagonistic to Christianity, the Author believes and seeks to shew that every new discovery tends more strongly to prove that Nature and the Bible have One Author. "Whether the reader agree or not with his conclusions, he will acknowledge he is in the presence of an original and thoughtful writer."—Pall Mall Gazette. *"There is no class of educated men and women that will not profit by these essays."*—Standard.

M'Cosh.—For Works by JAMES McCOSH, LL.D., President of Princeton College, New Jersey, U.S., *see* PHILOSOPHICAL CATALOGUE.

Maurice.—Works by the late Rev. F. DENISON MAURICE, M.A., Professor of Moral Philosophy in the University of Cambridge.

Professor Maurice's Works are recognized as having made a deep impression on modern theology. With whatever subject he dealt he tried to look at it in its bearing on living men and their everyday surroundings, and faced unshrinkingly the difficulties which occur to ordinary earnest thinkers in a manner that showed he had intense sympathy with all that concerns humanity. By all who wish to understand the various drifts of thought during the present century, Mr. Maurice's works must be studied. An intimate friend of Mr. Maurice's, one who has carefully studied all his works, and had besides many opportunities of knowing the Author's opinions, in speaking of his so-called "obscurity," ascribes it to "the never-failing assumption that God is really moving, teaching and acting; and that the writer's business is not so much to state something for the reader's benefit, as to apprehend what God is saying or doing." The Spectator *says—"Few of those of our own generation whose names will live in English history or literature have exerted so profound and so permanent an influence as Mr. Maurice."*

THE PATRIARCHS AND LAWGIVERS OF THE OLD TESTAMENT. Third and Cheaper Edition. Crown 8vo. 5s.

The Nineteen Discourses contained in this volume were preached in the chapel of Lincoln's Inn during the year 1851. *The texts are taken from the books of Genesis, Exodus, Numbers, Deuteronomy, Joshua, Judges, and Samuel, and involve some of the most interesting biblical topics discussed in recent times.*

THE PROPHETS AND KINGS OF THE OLD TESTAMENT. Third Edition, with new Preface. Crown 8vo. 10s. 6d.

The previous work brings down Old Testament history to the time of Samuel. The Sermons contained in the present volume—twenty-seven in number, coming down to the time of Ezekiel—though they

Maurice (F. D.)—*continued.*

commence at that point are distinct in their subject and treatment. Mr. Maurice, in the spirit which animated the compilers of the Church Lessons, has in these Sermons regarded the Prophets more as preachers of righteousness than as mere predictors—an aspect of their lives which, he thinks, has been greatly overlooked in our day, and than which, there is none we have more need to contemplate. He has found that the Old Testament Prophets, taken in their simple natural sense, clear up many of the difficulties which beset us in the daily work of life; make the past intelligible, the present endurable, and the future real and hopeful.

THE GOSPEL OF THE KINGDOM OF HEAVEN.
A Series of Lectures on the Gospel of St. Luke. Crown 8vo. 9s.

Mr. Maurice, in his Preface to these Twenty-eight Lectures, says,—"*In these Lectures I have endeavoured to ascertain what is told us respecting the life of Jesus by one of those Evangelists who proclaim Him to be the Christ, who says that He did come from a Father, that He did baptize with the Holy Spirit, that He did rise from the dead. I have chosen the one who is most directly connected with the later history of the Church, who was not an Apostle, who professedly wrote for the use of a man already instructed in the faith of the Apostles. I have followed the course of the writer's narrative, not changing it under any pretext. I have adhered to his phraseology, striving to avoid the substitution of any other for his.*"

THE GOSPEL OF ST. JOHN. A Series of Discourses.
Third and Cheaper Edition. Crown 8vo. 6s.

These Discourses, twenty-eight in number, are of a nature similar to those on the Gospel of St. Luke, and will be found to render valuable assistance to any one anxious to understand the Gospel of the beloved disciple, so different in many respects from those of the other three Evangelists. Appended are eleven notes illustrating various points which occur throughout the discourses. The Literary Churchman *thus speaks of this volume:*—"*Thorough honesty, reverence, and deep thought pervade the work, which is every way*

Maurice (F. D.)—*continued.*

solid and philosophical, as well as theological, and abounding with suggestions which the patient student may draw out more at length for himself."

THE EPISTLES OF ST. JOHN. A Series of Lectures on Christian Ethics. Second and Cheaper Edition. Cr. 8vo. 6s.

These Lectures on Christian Ethics were delivered to the students of the Working Men's College, Great Ormond Street, London, on a series of Sunday mornings. There are twenty Lectures in all, founded on various texts taken from the Epistles of St. John, which abound in passages bearing directly on the conduct of life, the duty of men to God and to each other. It will be found that a very complete system of practical morality is developed in this volume, in which the most important points in Ethics are set forth in an unconventional and interesting manner. Mr. Maurice believes that the question in which we are most interested, the question which most affects our studies and our daily lives, is the question, whether there is a foundation for human morality, or whether it is dependent upon the opinions and fashions of different ages and countries. This important question will be found amply and fairly discussed in this volume, which the National Review *calls "Mr. Maurice's most effective and instructive work. He is peculiarly fitted by the constitution of his mind, to throw light on St. John's writings." Appended is a note on "Positivism and its Teacher."*

EXPOSITORY SERMONS ON THE PRAYER-BOOK. The Prayer-book considered especially in reference to the Romish System. Second Edition. Fcap. 8vo. 5s. 6d.

After an Introductory Sermon, Mr. Maurice goes over the various parts of the Church Service, expounds in eighteen Sermons, their intention and significance, and shews how appropriate they are as expressions of the deepest longings and wants of all classes of men.

LECTURES ON THE APOCALYPSE, or Book of the Revelation of St. John the Divine. Crown 8vo. 10s. 6d.

These Twenty-three Lectures on what is generally regarded as the most

Maurice (F. D.)—*continued.*

mysterious Book in the Bible, do not demand that extensive knowledge of ancient or modern history which it is necessary to possess to be able to judge of most modern commentaries on Prophecy. Mr. Maurice, instead of trying to find far-fetched allusions to great historical events in the distant future, endeavours to discover the plain, literal, obvious meaning of the words of the writer, and shews that as a rule these refer to events contemporaneous with or immediately succeeding the time when the book was written. At the same time he shews the applicability of the contents of the book to the circumstances of the present day and of all times. "Never," says the Nonconformist, "has Mr. Maurice been more reverent, more careful for the letter of the Scripture, more discerning of the purpose of the Spirit, or more sober and practical in his teaching, than in this volume on the Apocalypse."*

WHAT IS REVELATION? A Series of Sermons on the Epiphany; to which are added, Letters to a Theological Student on the Bampton Lectures of Mr. Mansel. Crown 8vo. 10s. 6d.

Both Sermons and Letters were called forth by the doctrine maintained by Mr. Mansel in his Bampton Lectures, that Revelation cannot be a direct Manifestation of the Infinite Nature of God. Mr. Maurice maintains the opposite doctrine, and in his Sermons explains why, in spite of the high authorities on the other side, he must still assert the principle which he discovers in the Services of the Church and throughout the Bible. In the Letters to a Student of Theology, he has followed out all Mr. Mansel's Statements and Arguments step by step. The Nonconformist says, "There will be found ample materials to stimulate Christian faith and earnestness, to quicken and give tenderness to charity, and to vivify conceptions of the 'things not seen which are eternal.'"

SEQUEL TO THE INQUIRY, "WHAT IS REVELATION?" Letters in Reply to Mr. Mansel's Examination of "Strictures on the Bampton Lectures." Crown 8vo. 6s.

This, as the title indicates, was called forth by Mr. Mansel's Examination of Mr. Maurice's Strictures on his doctrine of the Infinite.

Maurice (F. D.)—*continued.*

THEOLOGICAL ESSAYS. Third Edition. Crown 8vo. 10s. 6d.

> "*The book,*" says Mr. Maurice, "*expresses thoughts which have been working in my mind for years; the method of it has not been adopted carelessly; even the composition has undergone frequent revision.*" *There are seventeen Essays in all, and although meant primarily for Unitarians, to quote the words of the* Clerical Journal, "*it leaves untouched scarcely any topic which is in agitation in the religious world; scarcely a moot point between our various sects; scarcely a plot of debateable ground between Christians and Infidels, between Romanists and Protestants, between Socinians and other Christians, between English Churchmen and Dissenters on both sides. Scarce is there a misgiving, a difficulty, an aspiration stirring amongst us now,—now, when men seem in earnest as hardly ever before about religion, and ask and demand satisfaction with a fearlessness which seems almost awful when one thinks what is at stake—which is not recognised and grappled with by Mr. Maurice.*"

THE DOCTRINE OF SACRIFICE DEDUCED FROM THE SCRIPTURES. Crown 8vo. 7s. 6d.

> *Throughout the Nineteen Sermons contained in this volume, Mr. Maurice expounds the ideas which he has formed of the Doctrine of Sacrifice, as it is set forth in various parts of the Bible.* " *The habitual tone,*" says the Christian Spectator, "*is that of great seriousness and calm,—a seriousness which makes an impression of its own, and a serenity which is only broken by some overpowering feeling forcing itself into expression, and making itself heard in most meaning and stirring words.*"

THE RELIGIONS OF THE WORLD, AND THEIR RELATIONS TO CHRISTIANITY. Fourth Edition. Fcap. 8vo. 5s.

> *These Eight Boyle Lectures are divided into two parts, of four Lectures each. In the first part Mr. Maurice examines the great Religious systems which present themselves in the history of the*

Maurice (F. D.)—*continued.*

world, with the purpose of inquiring what is their main characteristic principle. The second four Lectures are occupied with a discussion of the questions, "In what relation does Christianity stand to these different faiths? If there be a faith which is meant for mankind, is this the one, or must we look for another?" In the Preface, the most important authorities on the various subjects discussed in the Lectures are referred to, so that the reader may pursue the subject further.

ON THE LORD'S PRAYER. Fourth Edition. Fcap. 8vo. 2s. 6d.

In these Nine Sermons the successive petitions of the Lord's Prayer are taken up by Mr. Maurice, their significance expounded, and, as was usual with him, connected with the every-day lives, feelings, and aspirations of the men of the present time. They were delivered in the momentous year 1848, *and frequent allusions are made and lessons drawn from the events of that year.*

ON THE SABBATH DAY; the Character of the Warrior, and on the Interpretation of History. Fcap. 8vo. 2s. 6d.

This volume contains Three Sermons on the Sabbath-day, one of them being in reference to the proposed opening of the Crystal Palace on Sunday—one on the "Character of the Warrior," suggested by the Death of the Duke of Wellington; the fifth being on "The Divine Interpretation of History," delivered during the Great Exhibition of 1851. *In this last Mr. Maurice points out a few difficulties which, judging from his own experience, he thinks likely to perplex students of history, explaining how the Bible has anticipated and resolved them.*

THE GROUND AND OBJECT OF HOPE FOR MANKIND. Four Sermons preached before the University of Cambridge. Crown 8vo. 3s. 6d.

In these Four Sermons Mr. Maurice views the subject in four aspects:—I. The Hope of the Missionary. II. The Hope of the Patriot. III. The Hope of the Churchman. IV. The Hope of

Maurice (F. D.)—*continued.*

Man. The Spectator *says,* "*It is impossible to find anywhere deeper teaching than this;*" *and the* Nonconformist, "*We thank him for the manly, noble, stirring words in these Sermons—words fitted to quicken thoughts, to awaken high aspiration, to stimulate to lives of goodness.*"

THE LORD'S PRAYER, THE CREED, AND THE COMMANDMENTS.
A Manual for Parents and Schoolmasters. To which is added the Order of the Scriptures. 18mo. cloth limp. 1s.

This book is not written for clergymen, as such, but for parents and teachers, who are often either prejudiced against the contents of the Catechism, or regard it peculiarly as the clergyman's book, but, at the same time, have a general notion that a habit of prayer ought to be cultivated, that there are some things which ought to be believed, and some things which ought to be done. It will be found to be peculiarly valuable at the present time, when the question of religious education is occupying so much attention.

THE CLAIMS OF THE BIBLE AND OF SCIENCE.
A Correspondence on some Questions respecting the Pentateuch. Crown 8vo. 4s. 6d.

This volume consists of a series of Fifteen Letters, the first and last addressed by a 'Layman' to Mr. Maurice, the intervening thirteen written by Mr. Maurice himself.

DIALOGUES ON FAMILY WORSHIP. Crown 8vo. 6s.

"*The parties in these Dialogues,*" *says the Preface,* "*are a Clergyman who accepts the doctrines of the Church, and a Layman whose faith in them is nearly gone. The object of the Dialogues is not confutation, but the discovery of a ground on which two Englishmen and two fathers may stand, and on which their country and their children may stand when their places know them no more.*" *Some of the most important doctrines of the Church are discussed, the whole series of dialogues tending to shew that men of all shades of belief may look up to and worship God as their common and loving Father.*

Maurice (F. D.)—*continued.*

THE COMMANDMENTS CONSIDERED AS INSTRUMENTS OF NATIONAL REFORMATION. Crown 8vo. 4s. 6d.

This is a book of practical morality and divinity. It was to some extent occasioned by Dr. Norman Macleod's Speech on the Sabbath, and his views of the Commandments. The author endeavours to shew that the Commandments are now, and ever have been, the great protesters against Presbyteral and Prelatical assumptions, and that if we do not receive them as Commandments of the Lord God spoken to Israel, and spoken to every people under heaven now, we lose the greatest witnesses we possess for national morality and civil freedom.

MORAL AND METAPHYSICAL PHILOSOPHY. Vol. I. Ancient Philosophy from the First to the Thirteenth Centuries. Vol. II. Fourteenth Century and the French Revolution, with a Glimpse into the Nineteenth Century. Two Vols. 8vo. 25s.

This is an edition in two volumes of Professor Maurice's History of Philosophy from the earliest period to the present time. It was formerly issued in a number of separate volumes, and it is believed that all admirers of the author and all students of philosophy will welcome this compact edition. In a long introduction to this edition, in the form of a dialogue, Professor Maurice justifies his own views, and touches upon some of the most important topics of the time.

SOCIAL MORALITY. Twenty-one Lectures delivered in the University of Cambridge. New and Cheaper Edition. Cr. 8vo. 10s. 6d.

In this series of Lectures, Professor Maurice considers, historically and critically, Social Morality in its three main aspects:—I. "The Relations which spring from the Family—Domestic Morality." II. "Relations which subsist among the various constituents of a Nation—National Morality." III. "As it concerns Universal Humanity—Universal Morality." Appended to each series is a chapter on "Worship;" first, "Family Worship;" second,

Maurice (F. D.)—*continued.*

"*National Worship;*" third, "*Universal Worship.*" "*Whilst reading it we are charmed by the freedom from exclusiveness and prejudice, the large charity, the loftiness of thought, the eagerness to recognise and appreciate whatever there is of real worth extant in the world, which animates it from one end to the other. We gain new thoughts and new ways of viewing things, even more, perhaps, from being brought for a time under the influence of so noble and spiritual a mind.*"—Athenæum.

THE CONSCIENCE: Lectures on Casuistry, delivered in the University of Cambridge. Second and Cheaper Edition. Crown 8vo. 5s.

In this series of nine Lectures, Professor Maurice, endeavours to settle what is meant by the word "Conscience," and discusses the most important questions immediately connected with the subject. Taking "Casuistry" in its old sense as being the "study of cases of Conscience," he endeavours to show in what way it may be brought to bear at the present day upon the acts and thoughts of our ordinary existence. He shows that Conscience asks for laws, not rules; for freedom, not chains; for education, not suppression. He has abstained from the use of philosophical terms, and has touched on philosophical systems only when he fancied "they were interfering with the rights and duties of wayfarers." The Saturday Review says: "We rise from the perusal of these lectures with a detestation of all that is selfish and mean, and with a living impression that there is such a thing as goodness after all."

LECTURES ON THE ECCLESIASTICAL HISTORY OF THE FIRST AND SECOND CENTURIES. 8vo. 10s. 6d.

The work contains a series of graphic sketches and vivid portraits, bringing forcibly before the reader the life of the early Church in all its main aspects. In the first chapter on "The Jewish Calling," besides expounding his idea of the true nature of a "Church," the author gives a brief sketch of the position and economy of the Jews; while in the second he points out their relation to "the other Nations." Chapter Third contains a succint account of the various Jewish

Maurice (F. D.)—*continued.*

Sects, while in Chapter Fourth are briefly set forth Mr. Maurice's ideas of the character of Christ and the nature of His mission, and a sketch of events is given up to the Day of Pentecost. The remaining Chapters, extending from the Apostles' personal Ministry to the end of the Second Century, contain sketches of the character and work of all the prominent men in any way connected with the Early Church, accounts of the origin and nature of the various doctrines orthordox and heretical which had their birth during the period, as well as of the planting and early history of the Chief Churches in Asia, Africa and Europe.

LEARNING AND WORKING. Six Lectures delivered in Willis's Rooms, London, in June and July, 1854.—THE RELIGION OF ROME, and its Influence on Modern Civilisation. Four Lectures delivered in the Philosophical Institution of Edinburgh, in December, 1854. Crown 8vo. 5s.

In the Dedication and Preface to this volume, Professor Maurice shows that these two sets of Lectures have many points of connection. In the first series of Lectures the author endeavours to explain to such an audience as was likely to meet in Willis's Rooms, the scope and aims of the course of education established at the then recently founded Working Men's College, and at the same time expounds his notions of education in general, the pivot of his system being the truth that Learning and Working are not incompatible. The title to the second series is a sufficient index to their nature.

Moorhouse.—Works by JAMES MOORHOUSE, M.A., Vicar of Paddington :—

SOME MODERN DIFFICULTIES RESPECTING the FACTS OF NATURE AND REVELATION. Fcap. 8vo. 2s. 6d.

The first of these Four Discourses is a systematic reply to the Essay of the Rev. Baden Powell on Christian Evidences in "Essays and Reviews." The fourth Sermon, on " The Resurrection," is in

Moorhouse (J.)—*continued.*

some measure complementary to this, and the two together are intended to furnish a tolerably complete view of modern objections to Revelation. In the second and third Sermons, on the "Temptation" and "Passion," the author has endeavoured "to exhibit the power and wonder of those great facts within the spiritual sphere, which modern theorists have especially sought to discredit." The British Quarterly *says of them,—"The tone of the discussion is able, and throughout conservative of Scriptural truth."*

JACOB. Three Sermons preached before the University of Cambridge in Lent 1870. Extra fcap. 8vo. 3s. 6d.

In these Three Sermons the author endeavours to indicate the course of that Divine training by which the patriarch Jacob was converted from a deceitful and unscrupulous into a pious and self-denying man. In the first Sermon is considered "The Human Subject," or the nature to be trained; in the second "The Divine Power," the power by which that training was effected; and in the third "The Great Change," or the course and form of the training.

THE HULSEAN LECTURES FOR 1865. Cr. 8vo. 5s.

The following are the subjects of the Four Hulsean Lectures in this volume:—I. "Bearing of Present Controversies on the Doctrine of the Incarnation." II. "How far the Hypothesis of a real Limitation in our Saviour's Human Knowledge is consistent with the Doctrine of His Divinity." III. "The Scriptural Evidence of our Saviour's Sinlessness." IV. "What Kind and Degree of Human Ignorance were left possible to our Lord Jesus Christ by the fact of His Human Sinlessness." "Few more valuable works have come into our hands for many years . . . a most fruitful and welcome volume."—Church Review.

O'Brien.—AN ATTEMPT TO EXPLAIN and ESTABLISH THE DOCTRINE OF JUSTIFICATION by FAITH ONLY. By JAMES THOMAS O'BRIEN, D.D., Bishop of Ossory. Third Edition. 8vo. 12s.

This work consists of Ten Sermons. The first four treat of the nature and mutual relations of Faith and Justification; the fifth and sixth examine the corruptions of the doctrine of Justification by Faith only, and the objections which have been urged against it. The four concluding sermons deal with the moral effects of Faith. Various Notes are added explanatory of the Author's reasoning.

Palgrave.—HYMNS. By FRANCIS TURNER PALGRAVE. Third Edition, enlarged. 18mo. 1s. 6d.

This is a collection of twenty original Hymns, which the Literary Churchman *speaks of as "so choice, so perfect, and so refined,— so tender in feeling, and so scholarly in expression."*

Palmer.—THE BOOK OF PRAISE: From the Best English Hymn Writers. Selected and arranged by Lord SELBORNE. With Vignette by WOOLNER. 18mo. 4s. 6d.

The present is an attempt to present, under a convenient arrangement, a collection of such examples of a copious and interesting branch of popular literature, as, after several years' study of the subject, have seemed to the Editor most worthy of being separated from the mass to which they belong. It has been the Editor's desire and aim to adhere strictly, in all cases in which it could be ascertained, to the genuine uncorrupted text of the authors themselves. The names of the authors and date of composition of the hymns, when known, are affixed, while notes are added to the volume, giving further details. The Hymns are arranged according to subjects. "There is not room for two opinions as to the value of the 'Book of Praise.'" —Guardian. *"Approaches as nearly as one can conceive to perfection."*—Nonconformist.

BOOK OF PRAISE HYMNAL. *See* end of this Catalogue.

Paul of Tarsus. An Inquiry into the Times and the Gospel of the Apostle of the Gentiles. By a GRADUATE. 8vo. 10s. 6d.

The Author of this work has attempted, out of the materials which were at his disposal, to construct for himself a sketch of the time in which St. Paul lived, of the religious systems with which he was brought in contact, of the doctrine which he taught, and of the work which he ultimately achieved. "Turn where we will throughout the volume, we find the best fruit of patient inquiry, sound scholarship, logical argument, and fairness of conclusion. No thoughtful reader will rise from its perusal without a real and lasting profit to himself, and a sense of permanent addition to the cause of truth."—Standard.

Prescott.—THE THREEFOLD CORD. Sermons preached before the University of Cambridge. By J. E. PRESCOTT, B.D. Fcap. 8vo. 3s. 6d.

The title of this volume is derived from the subjects of the first three of these Sermons—Love, Hope, Faith. Their full titles are:—I. "Christ the Bringer of Peace—Love." II. "Christ the Renovator—Hope." III. "Christ the Light—Faith." The fourth, an Assize Sermon, is on "The Divinity of Justice." The Sermons are an attempt to shew that Christian theology is sufficient for the wants of the present day.

Procter.—A HISTORY OF THE BOOK OF COMMON PRAYER: With a Rationale of its Offices. By FRANCIS PROCTER, M.A. Tenth Edition, revised and enlarged. Crown 8vo. 10s. 6d.

The fact that in fifteen years nine editions of this volume have been called for, shews that such a work was wanted, and that to a large extent Mr. Procter's book has supplied the want. "In the course of the last thirty years," the author says, "the whole subject has been investigated by divines of great learning, and it was mainly with a view of epitomizing their extensive publications, and correcting by their help sundry traditional errors or misconceptions, that the present volume was put together." The Second Part is occupied with an account of "The Sources and Rationale of the Offices." The Athenæum *says:—"The origin of every part of the Prayer-book has been diligently investigated,—and there are few questions or facts connected with it which are not either sufficiently explained, or so referred to, that persons interested may work out the truth for themselves."*

Procter and Maclear.—AN ELEMENTARY INTRODUCTION TO THE BOOK OF COMMON PRAYER. Fourth Edition, Re-arranged and Supplemented by an Explanation of the Morning and Evening Prayer and the Litany. By F. PROCTER, M.A. and G. F. MACLEAR, D.D. 18mo. 2s. 6d.

This book has the same object and follows the same plan as the Manuals already noticed under Mr. Maclear's name. Each book is subdivided into chapters and sections. In Book I. is given a detailed History of the Book of Common Prayer down to the Attempted Revision in the Reign of William III. Book II., consisting of four Parts, treats in order the various parts of the Prayer Book. Valuable Notes, etymological, historical, and critical, are given throughout the book, while the Appendix contains several articles of much interest and importance. Appended is a General Index and an Index of Words explained in the Notes. The Literary Churchman *characterizes it as "by far the completest and most satisfactory book of its kind we know. We wish it were in the hands of every schoolboy and every schoolmaster in the kingdom."*

Psalms of David CHRONOLOGICALLY ARRANGED. An Amended Version, with Historical Introductions and Explanatory Notes. By FOUR FRIENDS. Second and Cheaper Edition, much enlarged. Crown 8vo. 8s. 6d.

One of the chief designs of the Editors, in preparing this volume, was to restore the Psalter as far as possible to the order in which the Psalms were written. They give the division of each Psalm into strophes, and of each strophe into the lines which composed it, and amend the errors of translation. In accomplishing this work they have mainly followed the guidance of Professor Henry Ewald. A Supplement contains the chief specimens of Hebrew Lyric poetry not included in the Book of Psalms. The Spectator *calls it "One of the most instructive and valuable books that have been published for many years."*

Golden Treasury Psalter.—THE STUDENT'S EDITION. Being an Edition with briefer Notes of the above. 18mo. 3s. 6d.

This volume will be found to meet the requirements of those who wish for a smaller edition of the larger work, at a lower price for family use, and for the use of younger pupils in Public Schools. The short notes which are appended to the volume will, it is hoped, suffice to make the meaning intelligible throughout. The aim of this edition is simply to put the reader as far as possible in possession of the plain meaning of the writer. "It is a gem," the Nonconformist *says.*

Ramsay.—THE CATECHISER'S MANUAL; or, the Church Catechism Illustrated and Explained, for the Use of Clergymen, Schoolmasters, and Teachers. By ARTHUR RAMSAY, M.A. Second Edition. 18mo. 1s. 6d.

This Manual, which is in the form of question and answer, is intended to afford full assistance both to learners and teachers, to candidates for Confirmation as well as to clergymen, in the understanding of the Church Catechism, and of all the matters referred to therein.

Rays of Sunlight for Dark Days. A Book of Selections for the Suffering. With a Preface by C. J. VAUGHAN, D.D. 18mo. Fifth Edition. 3s. 6d. Also in morocco, old style.

Dr. Vaughan says in the Preface, after speaking of the general run of Books of Comfort for Mourners, "It is because I think that the little volume now offered to the Christian sufferer is one of greater wisdom and of deeper experience, that I have readily consented to the request that I would introduce it by a few words of Preface." The book consists of a series of very brief extracts from a great variety of authors, in prose and poetry, suited to the many moods of a mourning or suffering mind. "Mostly gems of the first water."—Clerical Journal.

Reynolds.—NOTES OF THE CHRISTIAN LIFE. A Selection of Sermons by HENRY ROBERT REYNOLDS, B.A., President of Cheshunt College, and Fellow of University College, London. Crown 8vo. 7s. 6d.

This work may be taken as representative of the mode of thought and feeling which is most popular amongst the freer and more cultivated

Nonconformists. *"The reader throughout,"* says the Patriot, *"feels himself in the grasp of an earnest and careful thinker."* *"It is long,"* says the Nonconformist, *"since we have met with any published sermons better calculated than these to stimulate devout thought, and to bring home to the soul the reality of a spiritual life."*

Roberts.—DISCUSSIONS ON THE GOSPELS. By the Rev. ALEXANDER ROBERTS, D.D. Second Edition, revised and enlarged. 8vo. 16s.

This volume is divided into two parts. Part I. "On the Language employed by our Lord and His Disciples," in which the author endeavours to prove that Greek was the language usually employed by Christ Himself, in opposition to the common belief that Our Lord spoke Aramæan. Part II. is occupied with a discussion "On the Original Language of St. Matthew's Gospel," and on "The Origin and Authenticity of the Gospels." "The author brings the valuable qualifications of learning, temper, and an independent judgment."—Daily News.

Robertson.—PASTORAL COUNSELS. Being Chapters on Practical and Devotional Subjects. By the late JOHN ROBERTSON, D.D. Third Edition, with a Preface by the Author of "The Recreations of a Country Parson." Extra fcap. 8vo. 6s.

These Sermons are the free utterances of a strong and independent thinker. He does not depart from the essential doctrines of his Church, but he expounds them in a spirit of the widest charity, and always having most prominently in view the requirements of practical life. "The sermons are admirable specimens of a practical, earnest, and instructive style of pulpit teaching."—Nonconformist.

Rowsell.—MAN'S LABOUR AND GOD'S HARVEST. Sermons preached before the University of Cambridge in Lent, 1861. Fcap. 8vo. 3s.

This volume contains Five Sermons, the general drift of which is indicated by the title. "We strongly recommend this little volume to young men, and especially to those who are contemplating work-

ing for Christ in Holy Orders."—Literary Churchman. *"Mr. Rowsell's Sermons must, we feel sure, have touched the heart of many a Cambridge Undergraduate, and are deserving of a wide general circulation."*—The Ecclesiastic.

Salmon.—THE REIGN OF LAW, and other Sermons, preached in the Chapel of Trinity College, Dublin. By the Rev. GEORGE SALMON, D.D., Regius Professor of Divinity in the University of Dublin. Crown 8vo. 6s.

Sanday.—THE AUTHORSHIP AND HISTORICAL CHARACTER OF THE FOURTH GOSPEL, considered in reference to the Contents of the Gospel itself. A Critical Essay. By WILLIAM SANDAY, M.A., Fellow of Trinity College, Oxford. Crown 8vo. 8s. 6d.

The object of this Essay is critical and nothing more. The Author attempts to apply faithfully and persistently to the contents of the much disputed fourth Gospel that scientific method which has been so successful in other directions. "The facts of religion," the Author believes, "(i. e. the documents, the history of religious bodies, &c.) are as much facts as the lie of a coal-bed or the formation of a coral-reef." "The Essay is not only most valuable in itself, but full of promise for the future."—Canon Westcott in the Academy.

Sergeant.—SERMONS. By the Rev. E. W. SERGEANT, M.A., Balliol College, Oxford; Assistant Master at Westminster College. Fcap. 8vo. 2s. 6d.

This volume contains Nine Sermons on a variety of topics, preached by the author at various times and to various classes of hearers. The First Sermon is on Free Inquiry.

Smith.—PROPHECY A PREPARATION FOR CHRIST. Eight Lectures preached before the University of Oxford, being the Bampton Lectures for 1869. By R. PAYNE SMITH, D.D., Dean of Canterbury. Second and Cheaper Edition. Crown 8vo. 6s.

The author's object in these Lectures is to shew that there exists in the

Old Testament an element, which no criticism on naturalistic principles can either account for or explain away: that element is Prophecy. The author endeavours to prove that its force does not consist merely in its predictions. The Bible describes man's first estate of innocency, his fall, and the promise given by God of his restoration. Virtually the promise meant that God would give man a true religion; and the author asserts that Christianity is the sole religion on earth that fulfils the conditions necessary to constitute a true religion. God has pledged His own attributes in its behalf; this pledge He has given in miracle and prophecy. The author endeavours to shew the reality of that portion of the proof founded on prophecy. "These Lectures overflow with solid learning."—Record.

Smith.—CHRISTIAN FAITH. Sermons preached before the University of Cambridge. By W. SAUMAREZ SMITH, M.A., Principal of St. Aidan's College, Birkenhead. Fcap. 8vo. 3s. 6d.

The first two sermons in this volume have special reference to the Person of Christ; the next two are concerned with the inner life of Christians; and the last speaks of the outward development of Christian faith. "Appropriate and earnest sermons, suited to the practical exhortation of an educated congregation."—Guardian.

Stanley.—Works by the Very Rev. A. P. STANLEY, D.D., Dean of Westminster.

THE ATHANASIAN CREED, with a Preface on the General Recommendations of the RITUAL COMMISSION. Cr. 8vo. 2s.

The object of the work is not so much to urge the omission or change of the Athanasian Creed, as to shew that such a relaxation ought to give offence to no reasonable or religious mind. With this view, the Dean of Westminster discusses in succession—(1) the Authorship of the Creed, (2) its Internal Characteristics, (3) the Peculiarities of its Use in the Church of England, (4) its Advantages and Disadvantages, (5) its various Interpretations, and (6) the Judgment passed upon it by the Ritual Commission. In conclusion, Dr. Stanley maintains that the use of the Athanasian

Stanley (Dean)—*continued.*

Creed should no longer be made compulsory. "*Dr. Stanley puts with admirable force the objections which may be made to the Creed; equally admirable, we think, in his statement of its advantages.*"—Spectator.

THE NATIONAL THANKSGIVING. Sermons preached in Westminster Abbey. Second Edition. Crown 8vo. 2s. 6d.

These Sermons are (1) "*Death and Life,*" *preached December* 10, 1871; (2) "*The Trumpet of Patmos,*" *December* 17, 1871; (3) "*The Day of Thanksgiving,*" *March* 3, 1872. *It is hoped that these Sermons may recall, in some degree, the serious reflections connected with the Prince of Wales's illness, which, if the nation is true to itself, ought not to perish with the moment. The proceeds of the publication will be devoted to the Fund for the Restoration of St. Paul's Cathedral.* "*In point of fervour and polish by far the best specimens in print of Dean Stanley's eloquent style.*"—Standard.

Sunday Library. See end of this Catalogue.

Swainson.—Works by C. A. SWAINSON, D.D., Canon of Chichester:—

THE CREEDS OF THE CHURCH IN THEIR RELATIONS TO HOLY SCRIPTURE and the CONSCIENCE OF THE CHRISTIAN. 8vo. cloth. 9s.

The Lectures which compose this volume discuss, amongst others, the following subjects: "*Faith in God,*" "*Exercise of our Reason,*" "*Origin and Authority of Creeds,*" *and* "*Private Judgment, its use and exercise.*" "*Treating of abstruse points of Scripture, he applies them so forcibly to Christian duty and practice as to prove eminently serviceable to the Church.*"—John Bull.

THE AUTHORITY OF THE NEW TESTAMENT, and other LECTURES, delivered before the University of Cambridge. 8vo. cloth. 12s.

The first series of Lectures in this work is on "*The Words spoken by* the Apostles of Jesus," "The Inspiration of God's Servants," "The Human Character of the Inspired Writers," and "The Divine Character of the Word written." The second embraces Lectures on "Sin as Imperfection," "Sin as Self-will," "Whatsoever is not of Faith is Sin," "Christ the Saviour," and "The Blood of the New Covenant." The third is on "Christians One Body in Christ," "The One Body the Spouse of Christ," "Christ's Prayer for Unity," "Our Reconciliation should be manifested in common Worship," and "Ambassadors for Christ." "All the grave and awful questions associated with human sinfulness and the Divine plan of redemption are discussed with minute and painstaking care, and in the Appendix all the passages of Scripture referring to them are marshalled and critically reviewed."—Wesleyan Times.

Taylor.—THE RESTORATION OF BELIEF. New and Revised Edition. By ISAAC TAYLOR, Esq. Crown 8vo. 8s. 6d.

The earlier chapters are occupied with an examination of the primitive history of the Christian Religion, and its relation to the Roman government; and here, as well as in the remainder of the work, the author shews the bearing of that history on some of the difficult and interesting questions which have recently been claiming the attention of all earnest men. The book will be found to contain a clear and full statement of the case as it at present stands in behalf of Christianity. The last chapter of this New Edition, treats of "The Present Position of the Argument concerning Christianity," with special reference to M. Renan's Vie de Jésus. *The* Journal of Sacred Literature *says,—"The current of thought which runs through this book is calm and clear, its tone is earnest, its manner courteous. The author has carefully studied the successive problems which he so ably handles."*

Temple.—SERMONS PREACHED IN THE CHAPEL of RUGBY SCHOOL. By F. TEMPLE, D.D., Bishop of Exeter. New and Cheaper Edition. Extra fcap. 8vo. 4s. 6d.

This volume contains Thirty-five Sermons on topics more or less intimately connected with every-day life. The following are a few of the subjects discoursed upon:—"Love and Duty;" "Coming to

Temple (F., D.D.)—*continued.*

Christ;" "Great Men;" "Faith;" "Doubts;" "Scruples;" "Original Sin;" "Friendship;" "Helping Others;" "The Discipline of Temptation;" "Strength a Duty;" "Worldliness;" "Ill Temper;" "The Burial of the Past." The Critic *speaks of them thus:—"We trust that the tender affectionate spirit of practical Christianity which runs through every page of the volume will have its due effect. . . . desiring to rouse the youthful hearers to a sense of duty, and to arm them against the perils and dangers of the world against which they are so soon to battle."*

A SECOND SERIES OF SERMONS PREACHED IN THE CHAPEL OF RUGBY SCHOOL. Second Edition. Extra fcap. 8vo. 6s.

This Second Series of Forty-two brief, pointed, practical Sermons, on topics intimately connected with the every-day life of young and old, will be acceptable to all who are acquainted with the First Series. The following are a few of the subjects treated of:—"Disobedience," "Almsgiving," "The Unknown Guidance of God," "Apathy one of our Trials," "High Aims in Leaders," "Doing our Best," "The Use of Knowledge," "Use of Observances," "Martha and Mary," "John the Baptist," "Severity before Mercy," "Even Mistakes Punished," "Morality and Religion," "Children," "Action the Test of Spiritual Life," "Self-Respect," "Too Late," "The Tercentenary."

A THIRD SERIES OF SERMONS PREACHED IN RUGBY SCHOOL CHAPEL IN 1867—1869. Extra fcap. 8vo. 6s.

This third series of Bishop Temple's Rugby Sermons, contains thirty-six brief discourses, characterized by "a penetrating and direct practicalness, informed by a rare intuitive sympathy with boy-nature; its keen perception of reality and earnestness, its equally keen sympathy with what is noblest in sentiment and feelings." The volume includes the "Good-bye" sermon preached on his leaving Rugby to enter on the office he now holds.

Thring.—Works by Rev. EDWARD THRING, M.A.
SERMONS DELIVERED AT UPPINGHAM SCHOOL.
Crown 8vo. 5s.

In this volume are contained Forty-seven brief Sermons, all on subjects more or less intimately connected with Public-school life. "We desire very highly to commend these capital Sermons which treat of a boy's life and trials in a thoroughly practical way and with great simplicity and impressiveness. They deserve to be classed with the best of their kind."—Literary Churchman.

THOUGHTS ON LIFE-SCIENCE. New Edition, enlarged and revised. Crown 8vo. 7s. 6d.

In this volume are discussed in a familiar manner some of the most interesting problems between Science and Religion, Reason and Feeling. "Learning and Science," says the Author, "are claiming the right of building up and pulling down everything, especially the latter. It has seemed to me no useless task to look steadily at what has happened, to take stock as it were of man's gains, and to endeavour amidst new circumstances to arrive at some rational estimate of the bearings of things, so that the limits of what is possible at all events may be clearly marked out for ordinary readers. .... This book is an endeavour, to bring out some of the main facts of the world."

Tracts for Priests and People. By VARIOUS WRITERS.
THE FIRST SERIES. Crown 8vo. 8s.
THE SECOND SERIES. Crown 8vo. 8s.

The whole Series of Fifteen Tracts may be had separately, price One Shilling each.

A series of papers written after the excitement aroused by the publication of "Essays and Reviews" had somewhat abated, and designed, by the exposition of positive truth, to meet the religious difficulties of honest inquirers. Amongst the writers are Mr. Thomas Hughes, Professor Maurice, the Rev. J. Llewellyn Davies, and Mr. J. M. Ludlow.

Trench.—Works by R. CHENEVIX TRENCH, D.D., Archbishop of Dublin. (For other Works by the same author, *see* BIOGRAPHICAL, BELLES LETTRES, and LINGUISTIC CATALOGUES).

Archbishop Trench is well known as a writer who has the happy faculty of being able to take with discrimination the results of the highest criticism and scholarship, and present them in such a shape as will be not only valuable to scholars, but interesting, intelligible, and of the greatest use even to the ordinary reader. It is generally acknowledged that few men have been more successful in bringing out the less obvious meanings of the New Testament, or done more for the popular yet scholarly exposition of the Bible generally.

NOTES ON THE PARABLES OF OUR LORD.
Eleventh Edition. 8vo. 12s.

This work has taken its place as a standard exposition and interpretation of Christ's Parables. The book is prefaced by an Introductory Essay in four chapters:—I. On the definition of the Parable. II. On Teaching by Parables. III. On the Interpretation of the Parables. IV. On other Parables besides those in the Scriptures. The author then proceeds to take up the Parables one by one, and by the aid of philology, history, antiquities, and the researches of travellers, shews forth the significance, beauty, and applicability of each, concluding with what he deems its true moral interpretation. In the numerous Notes are many valuable references, illustrative quotations, critical and philological annotations, etc., and appended to the volume is a classified list of fifty-six works on the Parables.

NOTES ON THE MIRACLES OF OUR LORD.
Ninth Edition. 8vo. 12s.

In the 'Preliminary Essay' to this work, all the momentous and interesting questions that have been raised in connection with Miracles, are discussed with considerable fulness, and the author's usual candour and learning. The Essay consists of six chapters: —I. On the Names of Miracles, i. e. the Greek words by which they are designated in the New Testament. II. The Miracles

Trench—*continued.*

and Nature—*What is the difference between a Miracle and any event in the ordinary course of Nature?* III. *The Authority of Miracles*—Is the Miracle to command absolute obedience? IV. *The Evangelical, compared with the other cycles of Miracles.* V. *The Assaults on the Miracles*—1. The Jewish. 2. The Heathen (Celsus etc.). 3. The Pantheistic (Spinoza etc.). 4. The Sceptical (Hume). 5. The Miracles only relatively miraculous (Schleiermacher). 6. The Rationalistic (Paulus). 7. The Historico-Critical (Woolston, Strauss). VI. *The Apologetic Worth of the Miracles.* The author then treats the separate Miracles as he does the Parables.

SYNONYMS OF THE NEW TESTAMENT. New Edition, enlarged. 8vo. cloth. 12s.

The study of synonyms in any language is valuable as a discipline for training the mind to close and accurate habits of thought; more especially is this the case in Greek—" *a language spoken by a people of the finest and subtlest intellect; who saw distinctions where others saw none; who divided out to different words what others often were content to huddle confusedly under a common term.* . . . *Where is it so desirable that we should miss nothing, that we should lose no finer intention of the writer, as in those words which are the vehicles of the very mind of God Himself?*" *This work is recognised as a valuable companion to every student of the New Testament in the original. This, the Seventh Edition, has been carefully revised, and a considerable number of new synonyms added. Appended is an Index to the Synonyms, and an Index to many other words alluded to or explained throughout the work.* "*He is,*" *the* Athenæum *says,* "*a guide in this department of knowledge to whom his readers may intrust themselves with confidence. His sober judgment and sound sense are barriers against the misleading influence of arbitrary hypotheses.*"

ON THE AUTHORIZED VERSION OF THE NEW TESTAMENT. Second Edition. 8vo. 7s.

Archbishop Trench's familiarity with the New Testament makes him peculiarly fitted to estimate the value of the present translation,

Trench—*continued.*

and to give directions as to how a new one should be proceeded with. After some Introductory Remarks, in which the propriety of a revision is briefly discussed, the whole question of the merits of the present version is gone into in detail, in eleven chapters. Appended is a chronological list of works bearing on the subject, an Index of the principal Texts considered, an Index of Greek Words, and an Index of other Words referred to throughout the book.

STUDIES IN THE GOSPELS. Second Edition. 8vo. 10s. 6d.

This book is published under the conviction that the assertion often made is untrue,—viz. that the Gospels are in the main plain and easy, and that all the chief difficulties of the New Testament are to be found in the Epistles. These "Studies," sixteen in number, are the fruit of a much larger scheme, and each Study deals with some important episode mentioned in the Gospels, in a critical, philosophical, and practical manner. Many learned references and quotations are added to the Notes. Among the subjects treated are:—The Temptation; Christ and the Samaritan Woman; The Three Aspirants; The Transfiguration; Zacchæus; The True Vine;. The Penitent Malefactor; Christ and the Two Disciples on the way to Emmaus.

COMMENTARY ON THE EPISTLES to the SEVEN CHURCHES IN ASIA. Third Edition, revised. 8vo. 8s. 6d.

The present work consists of an Introduction, being a commentary on Rev. i. 4—20, a detailed examination of each of the Seven Epistles, in all its bearings, and an Excursus on the Historico-Prophetical Interpretation of the Epistles.

THE SERMON ON THE MOUNT. An Exposition drawn from the writings of St. Augustine, with an Essay on his merits as an Interpreter of Holy Scripture. Third Edition, enlarged. 8vo. 10s. 6d.

The first half of the present work consists of a dissertation in eight chapters on "Augustine as an Interpreter of Scripture," the titles

Trench—*continued.*

of the several chapters being as follow:—*I. Augustine's General Views of Scripture and its Interpretation. II. The External Helps for the Interpretation of Scripture possessed by Augustine. III. Augustine's Principles and Canons of Interpretation. IV. Augustine's Allegorical Interpretation of Scripture. V. Illustrations of Augustine's Skill as an Interpreter of Scripture. VI. Augustine on John the Baptist and on St. Stephen. VII. Augustine on the Epistle to the Romans. VIII. Miscellaneous Examples of Augustine's Interpretation of Scripture. The latter half of the work consists of Augustine's Exposition of the Sermon on the Mount, not however a mere series of quotations from Augustine, but a connected account of his sentiments on the various passages of that Sermon, interspersed with criticisms by Archbishop Trench.*

SERMONS PREACHED in WESTMINSTER ABBEY.
Second Edition. 8vo. 10s. 6d.

These Sermons embrace a wide variety of topics, and are thoroughly practical, earnest, and evangelical, and simple in style. The following are a few of the subjects:—"*Tercentenary Celebration of Queen Elizabeth's Accession;*" "*Conviction and Conversion;*" "*The Incredulity of Thomas;*" "*The Angels' Hymn;*" "*Counting the Cost;*" "*The Holy Trinity in Relation to our Prayers;*" "*On the Death of General Havelock;*" "*Christ Weeping over Jerusalem;*" "*Walking with Christ in White.*"

SHIPWRECKS OF FAITH. Three Sermons preached before the University of Cambridge in May, 1867. Fcap. 8vo. 2s. 6d.

These Sermons are especially addressed to young men. The subjects are "*Balaam,*" "*Saul,*" *and* "*Judas Iscariot,*" *three of the mournfullest lives recorded in Scripture,* "*for the greatness of their vocation, and their disastrous falling short of the same, for the utter defeat of their lives, for the shipwreck of everything which they made.*" *These lives are set forth as beacon-lights,* "*to warn us off from perilous reefs and quicksands, which have been the destruction of many, and which might only too easily be*

Trench—*continued.*

ours." *The* John Bull *says,* "*they are, like all he writes, affectionate and earnest discourses.*"

SERMONS Preached for the most part in Ireland. 8vo. 10*s*. 6*d*.

This volume consists of Thirty-two Sermons, the greater part of which were preached in Ireland; the subjects are as follows:— Jacob, a Prince with God and with Men—Agrippa—The Woman that was a Sinner—Secret Faults—The Seven Worse Spirits— Freedom in the Truth—Joseph and his Brethren—Bearing one another's Burdens—Christ's Challenge to the World—The Love of Money—The Salt of the Earth—The Armour of God—Light in the Lord—The Jailer of Philippi—The Thorn in the Flesh— Isaiah's Vision—Selfishness—Abraham interceding for Sodom— Vain Thoughts—Pontius Pilate—The Brazen Serpent—The Death and Burial of Moses—A Word from the Cross—The Church's Worship in the Beauty of Holiness—Every Good Gift from Above —On the Hearing of Prayer—The Kingdom which cometh not with Observation—Pressing towards the Mark—Saul—The Good Shepherd—The Valley of Dry Bones—All Saints.

Tudor.—The DECALOGUE VIEWED as the CHRISTIAN'S LAW. With Special Reference to the Questions and Wants of the Times. By the Rev. RICH. TUDOR, B.A. Crown 8vo. 10*s*. 6*d*.

The author's aim is to bring out the Christian sense of the Decalogue in its application to existing needs and questions. The work will be found to occupy ground which no other single work has hitherto filled. It is divided into Two Parts, the First Part consisting of three lectures on "Duty," and the Second Part of twelve lectures on the Ten Commandments. The Guardian *says of it,* "*His volume throughout is an outspoken and sound exposition of Christian morality, based deeply upon true foundations, set forth systematically, and forcibly and plainly expressed—as good a specimen of what pulpit lectures ought to be as is often to be found.*"

Tulloch.—THE CHRIST OF THE GOSPELS AND THE CHRIST OF MODERN CRITICISM. Lectures on M. RENAN's "Vie de Jésus." By JOHN TULLOCH, D.D., Principal of the College of St. Mary, in the University of St. Andrew's. Extra fcap. 8vo. 4s. 6d.

While Dr. Tulloch does not hesitate to grapple boldly with the statements and theories of Renan, he does so in a spirit of perfect fairness and courtesy, eschewing all personalities and sinister insinuations as to motives and sincerity. The work will be found to be a fair and full statement, in Dr. Tulloch's eloquent style, of the case as it stands against Renan's theory.

Vaughan.—Works by CHARLES J. VAUGHAN, D.D., Master of the Temple:—

Dr. Vaughan's genuine sympathy with the difficulties, sorrows and struggles of all classes of his fellow-men, his thorough disinterestedness, and his high views of life have been acknowledged by critics of all creeds. No sermons can be more applicable to the ever-recurring ills, bodily, mental, and spiritual, that flesh is heir to. His commentaries and expository lectures are those of a faithful evangelical, but at the same time liberal-minded interpreter of what he believes to be the Word of God.

CHRIST SATISFYING THE INSTINCTS OF HUMANITY. Eight Lectures delivered in the Temple Church. Extra fcp. 8vo. 3s. 6d.

The object of these Sermons is to exhibit the spiritual wants of human nature, and to prove that all of them receive full satisfaction in Christ. The various instincts which He is shewn to meet are those of Truth, Reverence, Perfection, Liberty, Courage, Sympathy, Sacrifice, and Unity. "We are convinced that there are congregations, in number unmistakeably increasing, to whom such Essays as these, full of thought and learning, are infinitely more beneficial, for they are more acceptable, than the recognised type of sermons." —John Bull.

Vaughan (Dr. C. J.)—*continued.*

MEMORIALS OF HARROW SUNDAYS. A Selection of Sermons preached in Harrow School Chapel. With a View of the Chapel. Fourth Edition. Crown 8vo. 10s. 6d.

While these Sermons deal with subjects that in a peculiar way concern the young, and in a manner that cannot fail to attract their attention and influence their conduct, they are in every respect applicable to people of all ages. "Discussing," says the John Bull, *"those forms of evil and impediments to duty which peculiarly beset the young, Dr. Vaughan has, with singular tact, blended deep thought and analytical investigation of principles with interesting earnestness and eloquent simplicity." The* Nonconformist *says "the volume is a precious one for family reading, and for the hand of the thoughtful boy or young man entering life."*

THE BOOK AND THE LIFE, and other Sermons, preached before the University of Cambridge. New Edition. Fcap. 8vo. 4s. 6d.

These Sermons are all of a thoroughly practical nature, and some of them are especially adapted to those who are in a state of anxious doubt. "They meet," the Freeman *says, "in what appears to us to be the one true method, the scepticism and indifference to religious truth which are almost sure to trouble young men who read and think. In short, we know no book more likely to do the young and inquiring good, or to help them to gain that tone of mind wanting which they may doubt and ask for ever, because always doubting and asking in vain."*

TWELVE DISCOURSES on SUBJECTS CONNECTED WITH THE LITURGY and WORSHIP of the CHURCH OF ENGLAND. Fcap. 8vo. 6s.

Four of these discourses were published in 1860, *in a work entitled* Revision of the Liturgy; *four others have appeared in the form of separate sermons, delivered on various occasions, and published at the time by request; and four are new. All will be found to*

Vaughan (Dr. C. J.)—*continued.*

fall strictly under the present title, reviewing the chief matters suggested by the Church Liturgy. The Appendix contains two articles,—one on "Subscription and Scruples," the other on the "Rubric and the Burial Service." The Press *characterises the volume as "eminently wise and temperate."*

LESSONS OF LIFE AND GODLINESS. A Selection of Sermons preached in the Parish Church of Doncaster. Fourth and Cheaper Edition. Fcap. 8vo. 3s. 6d.

This volume consists of Nineteen Sermons, mostly on subjects connected with the every-day walk and conversation of Christians. They bear such titles as "The Talebearer," "Features of Charity," "The Danger of Relapse," "The Secret Life and the Outward," "Family Prayer," "Zeal without Consistency," "The Gospel an Incentive to Industry in Business," "Use and Abuse of the World." The Spectator *styles them "earnest and human. They are adapted to every class and order in the social system, and will be read with wakeful interest by all who seek to amend whatever may be amiss in their natural disposition or in their acquired habits."*

WORDS FROM THE GOSPELS. A Second Selection of Sermons preached in the Parish Church of Doncaster. Second Edition. Fcap. 8vo. 4s. 6d.

In this volume are Twenty-two Sermons on subjects taken from one or other of the four Gospels. The Nonconformist *characterises these Sermons as "of practical earnestness, of a thoughtfulness that penetrates the common conditions and experiences of life, and brings the truths and examples of Scripture to bear on them with singular force, and of a style that owes its real elegance to the simplicity and directness which have fine culture for their roots.... A book than which few could give more holy pleasantness and solemn purpose to their Sabbath evenings at home."*

Vaughan (Dr. C. J.)—*continued.*

LESSONS OF THE CROSS AND PASSION. Six Lectures delivered in Hereford Cathedral during the Week before Easter, 1869. Fcap. 8vo. 2s. 6d.

This volume contains Six Sermons on subjects mainly connected with the death and passion of Christ. The titles of the Sermons are:—I. "Too Late" (Matt. xxvi. 45). II. "The Divine Sacrifice and the Human Priesthood." III. "Love not the World." IV. "The Moral Glory of Christ." V. "Christ made perfect through Suffering." VI. "Death the Remedy of Christ's Loneliness." "This little volume," the Nonconformist *says, "exhibits all his best characteristics. Elevated, calm, and clear, the Sermons owe much to their force, and yet they seem literally to owe nothing to it. They are studied, but their grace is the grace of perfect simplicity."*

LIFE'S WORK AND GOD'S DISCIPLINE. Three Sermons. Fcap. 8vo. cloth. 2s. 6d.

The Three Sermons contained in this volume have a oneness of aim indicated by the title, and are on the following subjects:—I. "The Work burned and the Workmen saved." II. "The Individual Hiring." III. "The Remedial Discipline of Disease and Death."

THE WHOLESOME WORDS OF JESUS CHRIST. Four Sermons preached before the University of Cambridge in November 1866. Second Edition. Fcap. 8vo. cloth. 3s. 6d.

Dr. Vaughan uses the word "Wholesome" here in its literal and original sense, the sense in which St. Paul uses it, as meaning healthy, sound, conducing to right living; and in these Sermons he points out and illustrates several of the "wholesome" characteristics of the Gospel,—the Words of Christ. The subjects of these Sermons are as follow:—I. "Naturalness and Spirituality of Revelation—Grandeur and Self-Control—Truthfulness and Tenderness." II. "Universality and Individuality of Christ's Gospel." III. "Oblivions and Ambitions of the Life of Grace." IV. "Regrets and Preparations of Human Life." The John Bull *says this volume is "replete with all the author's well-known vigour of thought and richness of expression."*

Vaughan (Dr. C. J.)—*continued.*

FOES OF FAITH. Sermons preached before the University of Cambridge in November 1868. Fcap. 8vo. 3*s.* 6*d.*

The "Foes of Faith" preached against in these Four Sermons are:— I. "Unreality." II. "Indolence." III. "Irreverence." IV. "Inconsistency,"—"Foes," says the author, "which must be manfully fought against by all who would be finally admitted into that holy communion and fellowship which is, for time and eternity, the blessed company of all faithful people." "They are written," the London Review *says, "with culture and elegance, and exhibit the thoughtful earnestness, piety, and good sense of their author."*

LECTURES ON THE EPISTLE to the PHILIPPIANS. Third and Cheaper Edition. Extra fcap. 8vo. 5*s.*

Each Lecture is prefaced by a literal translation from the Greek of the paragraph which forms its subject, contains first a minute explanation of the passage on which it is based, and then a practical application of the verse or clause selected as its text. The Press *speaks of these Lectures thus:—"Replete with good sense and practical religious advice... The language of the Apostle assumes a practical significance, which it seldom wears in the eyes of any ordinary reader, and Dr. Vaughan's listeners would feel themselves placed in the position of men receiving inspired instruction on the ordinary business of life. We can scarcely praise this plan too highly."*

LECTURES ON THE REVELATION OF ST. JOHN. Third and Cheaper Edition. Two Vols. Extra fcap. 8vo. 9*s.*

In this the Third Edition of these Lectures, the literal translations of the passages expounded will be found interwoven in the body of the Letures themselves. In attempting to expound this most-hard-to-understand Book, Dr. Vaughan, while taking from others what assistance he required, has not adhered to any particular school of interpretation, but has endeavoured to shew forth the significance of this Revelation by the help of his strong common

Vaughan (Dr. C. J.)—*continued.*

sense, critical acumen, scholarship, and reverent spirit. "*Dr. Vaughan's Sermons,*" *the* Spectator *says,* "*are the most practical discourses on the Apocalypse with which we are acquainted.*" *Prefixed is a Synopsis of the Book of Revelation, and appended is an Index of passages illustrating the language of the Book.*

EPIPHANY, LENT, AND EASTER. A Selection of Expository Sermons. Third Edition. Crown 8vo. 10s. 6d.

The first eighteen of these Sermons were preached during the seasons of 1860, *indicated in the title, and are practical expositions of passages taken from the lessons of the days on which they were delivered. The last eight Sermons were added to the Second Edition. As in the case of the Lectures on Philippians, each Lecture is prefaced with a careful and literal rendering of the original of the passage of which the Lecture is an exposition. The* Nonconformist *says that* "*in simplicity, dignity, close adherence to the words of Scripture, insight into 'the mind of the Spirit,' and practical thoughtfulness, they are models of that species of pulpit instruction to which they belong.*"

THE EPISTLES OF ST. PAUL. For English Readers. PART I., containing the FIRST EPISTLE TO THE THESSALONIANS. Second Edition. 8vo. 1s. 6d. Each Epistle will be published separately in its chronological order.

It is the object of this work to enable English readers, unacquainted with Greek, to enter with intelligence into the meaning, connection, and phraseology of the writings of the great Apostle. (1) *Each Epistle will be prefaced by an Introduction containing information as to the circumstances, design, and order of its composition.* (2) *The Authorized English Version occupies the foremost place in each page.* (3) *Beside it, in smaller type, is a literal English Version, made from the original Greek.* (4) *A free paraphrase stands below, in which it is attempted to express the sense and connection of the Epistle.* (5) *The Notes include both doctrinal explanation and verbal illustration; occasionally a brief word of application has been introduced.*

Vaughan (Dr. C. J.)—*continued*.

ST. PAUL'S EPISTLE TO THE ROMANS. The Greek Text, with English Notes. Third Edition, greatly enlarged. Crown 8vo. 7s. 6d.

This volume contains the Greek Text of the Epistle to the Romans as settled by the Rev. B. F. Westcott, D.D., for his complete recension of the Text of the New Testament. Appended to the text are copious critical and exegetical Notes, the result, of almost eighteen years' study on the part of the author. The "Index of Words illustrated or explained in the Notes" will be found, in some considerable degree, an Index to the Epistles as a whole. "I have desired," the author says, *"to catch and to represent the meaning of each passage and of the whole, without deriving it from any secondary source. One of my principal endeavours has been, to trace through the New Testament the uses of the more remarkable words or phrases which occur in the Epistle, arranging them, where the case required it, under their various modifications of sense." Prefixed to the volume is a discourse on "St. Paul's Conversion and Doctrine," suggested by some recent publications on St. Paul's theological standing. In the Preface to the Third Edition, which has been almost entirely rewritten, among other things, is a Synopsis of the contents of the Epistle. The* Guardian *says of the work,—"For educated young men his commentary seems to fill a gap hitherto unfilled... As a whole, Dr. Vaughan appears to us to have given to the world a valuable book of original and careful and earnest thought bestowed on the accomplishment of a work which will be of much service and which is much needed."*

THE CHURCH OF THE FIRST DAYS.

Series I. The Church of Jerusalem. Third Edition.
" II. The Church of the Gentiles. Second Edition.
" III. The Church of the World. Second Edition.

Fcap. 8vo. cloth. 4s. 6d. each.

The work is in three volumes:—I. "The Church of Jerusalem," extending from the 1st to the 8th chapter (inclusive) of the Acts. *II. "The Church of the Gentiles," from the 9th to the 16th chapter. III. "The Church of the World," from the 17th to the 28th chapter. Where necessary, the Authorized Version has been*

Vaughan (Dr. C. J.)—*continued.*

departed from, and a new literal translation taken as the basis of exposition. All possible topographical and historical light has been brought to bear on the subject; and while thoroughly practical in their aim, these Lectures will be found to afford a fair notion of the history and condition of the Primitive Church. The British Quarterly *says,—" These Sermons are worthy of all praise, and are models of pulpit teaching."*

COUNSELS for YOUNG STUDENTS. Three Sermons preached before the University of Cambridge at the Opening of the Academical Year 1870-71. Fcap. 8vo. 2s. 6d.

The titles of the Three Sermons contained in this volume are:—I. "The Great Decision." II. "The House and the Builder." III. "The Prayer and the Counter-Prayer." They all bear pointedly, earnestly, and sympathisingly upon the conduct and pursuits of young students and young men generally, to counsel whom, Dr. Vaughan's qualifications and aptitude are well known.

NOTES FOR LECTURES ON CONFIRMATION, with suitable Prayers. Eighth Edition. Fcap. 8vo. 1s. 6d.

In preparation for the Confirmation held in Harrow School Chapel, Dr. Vaughan was in the habit of printing week by week, and distributing among the Candidates, somewhat full notes of the Lecture he purposed to deliver to them, together with a form of Prayer adapted to the particular subject. He has collected these weekly Notes and Prayers into this little volume, in the hope that it may assist the labours of those who are engaged in preparing Candidates for Confirmation, and who find it difficult to lay their hand upon any one book of suitable instruction. The Press *says the work "commends itself at once by its simplicity and by its logical arrangement.... While points of doctrine, as they arise, are not lost sight of, the principal stress is laid on the preparation of the heart rather than the head."*

THE TWO GREAT TEMPTATIONS. The Temptation of Man, and the Temptation of Christ. Lectures delivered in the Temple Church, Lent 1872. Extra fcap. 8vo. 3s. 6d.

Vaughan.—Works by DAVID J. VAUGHAN, M.A., Vicar of St. Martin's, Leicester :—

SERMONS PREACHED IN ST. JOHN'S CHURCH, LEICESTER, during the Years 1855 and 1856. Crown 8vo. 5s. 6d.

These Twenty-five Sermons embrace a great variety of topics, all of the highest interest, are thoroughly practical in their nature, and calculated to give a hopeful view of life as seen in the light shed upon it by Christianity.

CHRISTIAN EVIDENCES AND THE BIBLE. New Edition, revised and enlarged. Fcap. 8vo. cloth. 5s. 6d.

The main object of this series of Twelve Sermons is to shew, that, quite irrespective of any theory as to the nature of the Bible and the special inspiration of its authors, there is good and sufficient reason for believing that Jesus Christ is the Son of God, who reveals and reconciles men to the Father. "This little volume," the Spectator *says, "is a model of that honest and reverent criticism of the Bible which is not only right, but the duty of English clergymen in such times as these to put forth from the pulpit."*

Venn.—ON SOME OF THE CHARACTERISTICS OF BELIEF, Scientific and Religious. Being the Hulsean Lectures for 1869. By the Rev. J. VENN, M.A. 8vo. 6s. 6d.

These discourses are intended to illustrate, explain, and work out into some of their consequences, certain characteristics by which the attainment of religious belief is prominently distinguished from the attainment of belief upon most other subjects.

Warington.—THE WEEK OF CREATION; OR, THE COSMOGONY OF GENESIS CONSIDERED IN ITS RELATION TO MODERN SCIENCE. By GEORGE WARINGTON, Author of "The Historic Character of the Pentateuch Vindicated." Crown 8vo. 4s. 6d.

The greater part of this work is taken up with the teaching of the Cosmogony. Its purpose is also investigated, and a chapter is devoted to the consideration of the passage in which the difficulties occur. *"A very able vindication of the Mosaic Cosmogony by a writer who unites the advantages of a critical knowledge of the Hebrew text and of distinguished scientific attainments."*—Spectator.

Westcott.—Works by BROOKE FOSS WESTCOTT, D.D., Regius Professor of Divinity in the University of Cambridge; Canon of Peterborough :—

The London Quarterly, *speaking of Mr. Westcott, says,—"To a learning and accuracy which command respect and confidence, he unites what are not always to be found in union with these qualities, the no less valuable faculties of lucid arrangement and graceful and facile expression."*

AN INTRODUCTION TO THE STUDY OF THE GOSPELS. Fourth Edition. Crown 8vo. 10s. 6d.

The author's chief object in this work has been to shew that there is a true mean between the idea of a formal harmonization of the Gospels and the abandonment of their absolute truth. After an Introduction on the General Effects of the course of Modern Philosophy on the popular views of Christianity, he proceeds to determine in what way the principles therein indicated may be applied to the study of the Gospels: The treatise is divided into eight Chapters:—I. The Preparation for the Gospel. II. The Jewish Doctrine of the Messiah. III. The Origin of the Gospels. IV. The Characteristics of the Gospels. V. The Gospel of St. John. VI. and VII. The Differences in detail and of arrangement in the Synoptic Evangelists. VIII. The Difficulties of the Gospels. The Appendices contain much valuable subsidiary matter.

A GENERAL SURVEY OF THE HISTORY OF THE CANON OF THE NEW TESTAMENT DURING THE FIRST FOUR CENTURIES. Third Edition, revised. Crown 8vo. 10s. 6d.

The object of this treatise is to deal with the New Testament as a whole, and that on purely historical grounds. The separate books

Westcott (Dr. B. F.)—*continued*.

of which it is composed are considered not individually, but as claiming to be parts of the apostolic heritage of Christians. The Author has thus endeavoured to connect the history of the New Testament Canon with the growth and consolidation of the Catholic Church, and to point out the relation existing between the amount of evidence for the authenticity of its component parts and the whole mass of Christian literature. "*The treatise*," says *the* British Quarterly, "*is a scholarly performance, learned, dispassionate, discriminating, worthy of his subject and of the present state of Christian literature in relation to it.*"

THE BIBLE IN THE CHURCH. A Popular Account of the Collection and Reception of the Holy Scriptures in the Christian Churches. Third Edition. 18mo. 4s. 6d.

The present volume has been written under the impression that a History of the whole Bible, and not of the New Testament only, would be required, if those unfamiliar with the subject were to be enabled to learn in what manner and with what consent the collection of Holy Scriptures was first made and then enlarged and finally closed by the Church. Though the work is intended to be simple and popular in its method, the author, for this very reason, has aimed at the strictest accuracy. The History of the Bible is brought down to the 16*th century, and the Appendix contains two articles,—I. "On the History of the Canon of the Old Testament before the Christian Era." II. "On the Contents of the most ancient MSS. of the Christian Bible." The* Literary Churchman *says, " Mr. Westcott's account of the 'Canon' is true history in the very highest sense."*

A GENERAL VIEW OF THE HISTORY OF THE ENGLISH BIBLE. Second Edition. Crown 8vo. 10s. 6d.

In the Introduction the author notices briefly the earliest vernacular versions of the Bible, especially those in Anglo-Saxon. Chapter I. is occupied with an account of the Manuscript English Bible from the 14*th century downwards; and in Chapter II. is narrated,*

Westcott (Dr. B. F.)—continued.

with many interesting personal and other details, the External History of the Printed Bible. In Chapter III. is set forth the Internal History of the English Bible, shewing to what extent the various English Translations were independent, and to what extent the translators were indebted to earlier English and foreign versions. In the Appendices, among other interesting and valuable matter, will be found "Specimens of the Earlier and Later Wycliffite Versions;" "Chronological List of Bibles;" "An Examination of Mr. Froude's History of the English Bible." The Pall Mall Gazette calls the work "A brief, scholarly, and, to a great extent, an original contribution to theological literature."

THE CHRISTIAN LIFE, MANIFOLD AND ONE.
Six Sermons preached in Peterborough Cathedral. Crown 8vo. 2s. 6d.

The Six Sermons contained in this volume are the first preached by the author as a Canon of Peterborough Cathedral. The subjects are:—I. "Life consecrated by the Ascension." II. "Many Gifts, One Spirit." III. "The Gospel of the Resurrection." IV. "Sufficiency of God." V. "Action the Test of Faith." VI. "Progress from the Confession of God." The Nonconformist calls them "Beautiful discourses, singularly devout and tender."

THE GOSPEL OF THE RESURRECTION.
Thoughts on its Relation to Reason and History. New Edition. Fcap. 8vo. 4s. 6d.

The present Essay is an endeavour to consider some of the elementary truths of Christianity, as a miraculous Revelation, from the side of History and Reason. The author endeavours to shew that a devout belief in the Life of Christ is quite compatible with a broad view of the course of human progress and a frank trust in the laws of our own minds. After a "Statement of the Question," and an Introduction on "Ideas of God, Nature, Miracles," Chapter I. treats of "The Resurrection and History;" Chapter II. "The Resurrection and Man;" Chapter III. "The Resurrection and the Church."—"We owe," the Patriot says, "Mr. Westcott a very

Westcott (Dr. B. F.)—*continued.*

great debt of gratitude for his very able little treatise, so faithful to the great truths which are so precious to us, so catholic and spiritual in its conceptions of these truths, and, moreover, so philosophical in analysis, organism, and presentation."

ON THE RELIGIOUS OFFICE OF THE UNIVERSITIES. [*In the Press.*

Wilkins.—THE LIGHT OF THE WORLD. An Essay, by A. S. WILKINS, M.A., Professor of Latin in Owens College, Manchester. Second Edition. Crown 8vo. 3s. 6d.

This is the Hulsean Prize Essay for 1869. *The subject proposed by the Trustees was,* "*The Distinctive Features of Christian as compared with Pagan Ethics.*" *This the author treats in six chapters:—I.* "*The Object and Scope of the Discussion.*" *II. and III.* "*Pagan Ethics—their Historical Development,*" *and their Greatest Perfection.*" *IV. V. and VI.* "*Christian Ethics —their Method,*" *their Perfection,*" *and their Power.*" *The author has tried to show that the Christian ethics so far transcend the ethics of any or all of the Pagan systems in method, in purity and in power, as to compel us to assume for them an origin, differing in kind from the origin of any purely human system.* "*It would be difficult to praise too highly the spirit, the burden, the conclusions, or the scholarly finish of this beautiful Essay.*"—British Quarterly Review.

Wilson.—RELIGIO CHEMICI. With a Vignette beautifully engraved after a Design by Sir NOEL PATON. By GEORGE WILSON, M.D. Crown 8vo. 8s. 6d.

"*George Wilson,*" *says the Preface to this volume,* "*had it in his heart for many years to write a book corresponding to the* Religio Medici *of Sir Thomas Browne, with the title* Religio Chemici. *Several of the Essays in this volume were intended to form chapters of it, but the health and leisure necessary to carry out his plans were never attainable, and thus fragments only of the designed work exist. These fragments, however, being in most cases like finished gems waiting to be set, some of them are now given in a collected form to his friends and the public."—"A more fascinating volume,"* the Spectator says, *"has seldom fallen into our hands."*

Wilson.—THE BIBLE STUDENT'S GUIDE TO THE MORE CORRECT UNDERSTANDING of the ENGLISH TRANSLATION OF THE OLD TESTAMENT, BY REFERENCE TO THE ORIGINAL HEBREW. By WILLIAM WILSON, D.D., Canon of Winchester. Second Edition, carefully revised. 4to. 25s.

"The author believes that the present work is the nearest approach to a complete Concordance of every word in the original that has yet been made: and as a Concordance, it may be found of great use to the Bible student, while at the same time it serves the important object of furnishing the means of comparing synonymous words, and of eliciting their precise and distinctive meaning. The knowledge of the Hebrew language is not absolutely necessary to the profitable use of the work; and it is believed that many devout and accurate students of the Bible, entirely unacquainted with it, will derive great advantage from frequent reference to these pages." Introductory to the body of the work, the author gives a sketch of the Construction of Hebrew. The plan of the work is simple: every word occurring in the English Version is arranged alphabetically, and under it is given the Hebrew word or words, with a full explanation of their meaning, of which it is meant to be a translation, and a complete list of the passages where it occurs. Following the general work is a complete Hebrew and English Index, which is, in effect, a Hebrew-English Dictionary. Appended are copious examples of the Figure Paronomasia, *which occurs so frequently in the Bible.*

Worship (The) of God and Fellowship among Men. Sermons on Public Worship. By Professor MAURICE, and others. Fcap. 8vo. 3s. 6d.

This volume consists of Six Sermons preached by various clergymen, and although not addressed specially to any class, were suggested by recent efforts to bring the members of the Working Class to our Churches. The preachers were—Professor Maurice, Rev. T. J. Rowsell, Rev. J. Ll. Davies, Rev. D. F. Vaughan. "They are very suggestive to those who may have to prepare sermons, and well calculated to be lent amongst the more thoughtful parishioners."—Literary Churchman.

Yonge (Charlotte M.)—SCRIPTURE READINGS for SCHOOLS AND FAMILIES. By CHARLOTTE M. YONGE, Author of "The Heir of Redclyffe." Globe 8vo. 1s. 6d. With Comments. 3s. 6d.

A SECOND SERIES. From Joshua to Solomon. Extra fcap. 8vo. 1s. 6d. With Comments. 3s. 6d.

Actual need has led the author to endeavour to prepare a reading book convenient for study with children, containing the very words of the Bible, with only a few expedient omissions, and arranged in Lessons of such length as by experience she has found to suit with children's ordinary power of accurate attentive interest. The verse form has been retained because of its convenience for children reading in class, and as more resembling their Bibles; but the poetical portions have been given in their lines. When Psalms or portions from the Prophets illustrate or fall in with the narrative, they are given in their chronological sequence. The Scripture portion, with a very few notes explanatory of mere words, is bound up apart to be used by children, while the same is also supplied with a brief comment, the purpose of which is either to assist the teacher in explaining the lesson, or to be used by more advanced young people to whom it may not be possible to give access to the authorities whence it has been taken. Professor Huxley at a meeting of the London School-board, particularly mentioned the Selection made by Miss Yonge, as an example of how selections might be made for School reading. "Her Comments are models of their kind."—Literary Churchman.

In crown 8vo. cloth extra, Illustrated, price 4s. 6d. each Volume; also kept in morocco and calf bindings at moderate prices, and in Ornamental Boxes containing Four Vols., 21s. each.

MACMILLAN'S SUNDAY LIBRARY.

A SERIES OF ORIGINAL WORKS BY EMINENT AUTHORS.

The Guardian *says*—"*All Christian households owe a debt of gratitude to Mr. Macmillan for that useful 'Sunday Library.'*"

THE FOLLOWING VOLUMES ARE NOW READY:—

The Pupils of St. John the Divine.—By CHARLOTTE M. YONGE, Author of "The Heir of Redclyffe."

The author first gives a full sketch of the life and work of the Apostle himself, drawing the material from all the most trustworthy authorities, sacred and profane; then follow the lives of his immediate disciples, Ignatius, Quadratus, Polycarp, and others; which are succeeded by the lives of many of their pupils. She then proceeds to sketch from their foundation the history of the many churches planted or superintended by St. John and his pupils, both in the East and West. In the last chapter is given an account of the present aspect of the Churches of St. John,—the Seven Churches of Asia mentioned in Revelations; also those of Athens, of Nîmes, of Lyons, and others in the West. "Young and old will be equally refreshed and taught by these pages, in which nothing is dull, and nothing is far-fetched."—Churchman.

The Hermits.—By Canon Kingsley.

The volume contains the lives of some of the most remarkable early Egyptian, Syrian, Persian, and Western hermits. The lives are mostly translations from the original biographies; "the reader will thus be able to see the men as wholes, to judge of their merits and defects."—"*It is from first to last a production full of interest, written with a liberal appreciation of what is memorable for good in the lives of the Hermits, and with a wise forbearance towards legends which may be due to the ignorance, and, no doubt, also to the strong faith of the early chroniclers."*—London Review.

Seekers after God.—By the Rev. F. W. Farrar, M.A., F.R.S., Head Master of Marlborough College.

In this volume the author seeks to record the lives, and gives copious samples of the almost Christ-like utterances of, with perhaps the exception of Socrates, "the best and holiest characters presented to us in the records of antiquity." They are Seneca, Epictetus, and Marcus Aurelius, most appropriately called "Seekers after God," seeing that "amid infinite difficulties and surrounded by a corrupt society, they devoted themselves to the earnest search after those truths which might best make their lives 'beautiful before God." The volume contains portraits of Aurelius, Seneca, and Antoninus Pius. "We can heartily recommend it as healthy in tone, instructive, interesting, mentally and spiritually stimulating and nutritious."—Nonconformist.

England's Antiphon.—By George Macdonald.

This volume deals chiefly with the lyric or song-form of English religious poetry, other kinds, however, being not infrequently introduced. The author has sought to trace the course of our religious poetry from the 13th to the 19th centuries, from before Chaucer to Tennyson. He endeavours to accomplish his object by selecting the men who have produced the finest religious poetry, setting forth the circumstances in which they were placed, characterising the men themselves, critically estimating their productions, and giving ample specimens of their best religious lyrics, and quotations from larger poems, illustrating the religious feeling of the poets or their times. "Dr. Macdonald has very successfully endeavoured to bring together in his little book a whole series of the sweet singers of England, and makes them raise, one after the other, their voices in praise of God."—Guardian.

Great Christians of France: ST. LOUIS and CALVIN. By M. GUIZOT.

From among French Catholics, M. Guizot has, in this volume, selected Louis, King of France in the 13th century, and among Protestants, Calvin the Reformer in the 16th century, "as two earnest and illustrious representatives of the Christian faith and life, as well as of the loftiest thought and purest morality of their country and generation." In setting forth with considerable fulness the lives of these prominent and representative Christian men, M. Guizot necessarily introduces much of the political and religious history of the periods during which they lived. "A very interesting book," says the Guardian.

Christian Singers of Germany.—By CATHERINE WINKWORTH.

In this volume the authoress gives an account of the principal hymn-writers of Germany from the 9th to the 19th century, introducing ample (altogether about 120 translations) specimens from their best productions. In the translations, while the English is perfectly idiomatic and harmonious, the characteristic differences of the poems have been carefully imitated, and the general style and metre retained. The book is divided into chapters, the writers noticed and the hymns quoted in each chapter, being representative of an epoch in the religious life of Germany. In thus tracing the course of German hymnology, the authoress is necessarily "brought into contact with those great movements which have stirred the life of the people."—"Miss Winkworth's volume of this series is, according to our view, the choicest production of her pen." —British Quarterly Review.

Apostles of Mediæval Europe.—By the Rev. G. F. MACLEAR, D.D., Head Master of King's College School, London.

In two Introductory Chapters the author notices some of the chief characteristics of the mediæval period itself; gives a graphic sketch of the devastated state of Europe at the beginning of that period, and an interesting account of the religions of the three great groups of vigorous barbarians—the Celts, the Teutons, and the Sclaves—who had, wave after wave, overflowed its surface. He then proceeds to sketch the lives and work of the chief of the courageous men who devoted themselves to the stupendous task of their conversion and civilization, during a period extending from the 5th to the 13th century; such as St. Patrick, St. Columba, St. Columbanus, St. Augustine of Canterbury, St. Boniface, St. Olaf, St. Cyril, Raymond Sull, and others. In narrating the lives of these men, many glimpses are given into the political, social, and religious life of Europe during the Middle Ages, and many interesting and instructive incidents are introduced. "Mr. Maclear will have done a great work if his admirable little volume shall help to break up the dense ignorance which is still prevailing among people at large."—Literary Churchman.

Alfred the Great.—By THOMAS HUGHES, M.P., Author of "Tom Brown's School Days." Third Edition.

" The time is come when we English can no longer stand by as interested spectators only, but in which every one of our institutions will be sifted with rigour, and will have to shew cause for its existence. . . . As a help in this search, this life of the typical English King is here offered." After two Introductory Chapters, one on Kings and Kingship, and another depicting the condition of Wessex when Alfred became its ruler, the author proceeds to set forth the life and work of this great prince, shewing how he conducted himself in all the relations of life. In the last chapter the author shews the bearing which Christianity has on the kingship and government of the nations and people of the world in which we live. Besides other illustrations in the volume, a Map of England is prefixed, shewing its divisions about 1000 A.D., *as well*

as at the present time. "*Mr. Hughes has indeed written a good book, bright and readable we need hardly say, and of a very considerable historical value.*"—Spectator.

Nations Around.—By Miss A. KEARY.

This volume contains many details concerning the social and political life, the religion, the superstitions, the literature, the architecture, the commerce, the industry, of the Nations around Palestine, an acquaintance with which is necessary in order to a clear and full understanding of the history of the Hebrew people. The authoress has brought to her aid all the most recent investigations into the early history of these nations, referring frequently to the fruitful excavations which have brought to light the ruins and hieroglyphic writings of many of their buried cities. "*Miss Keary has skilfully availed herself of the opportunity to write a pleasing and instructive book.*"—Guardian. "*A valuable and interesting volume.*"—Illustrated Times.

St. Anselm.—By the Very Rev. R. W. CHURCH, M.A., Dean of St. Paul's. Second Edition.

In this biography of St. Anselm, while the story of his life as a man, a Christian, a clergyman, and a politician, is told impartially and fully, much light is shed on the ecclesiastical and political history of the time during which he lived, and on the internal economy of the monastic establishments of the period. Of the worthiness of St. Anselm to have his life recorded, Mr. Church says, "*It would not be easy to find one who so joined the largeness and daring of a powerful and inquiring intellect, with the graces and sweetness and unselfishness of the most loveable of friends, and with the fortitude, clear-sightedness, and dauntless firmness of a hero, forced into a hero's career in spite of himself.*" *The author has drawn his materials from contemporary biographers and chroniclers, while at the same time he has consulted the best recent authors who have treated of the man and his time.* "*It is a sketch by the hand of a master, with every line marked by taste, learning, and real apprehension of the subject.*" — Pall Mall Gazette.

Francis of Assisi.—By Mrs. OLIPHANT.

The life of this saint, the founder of the Franciscan order, and one of the most remarkable men of his time, illustrates some of the chief characteristics of the religious life of the Middle Ages. Much information is given concerning the missionary labours of the saint and his companions, as well as concerning the religious and monastic life of the time. Many graphic details are introduced from the saint's contemporary biographers, which shew forth the prevalent beliefs of the period; and abundant samples are given of St. Francis's own sayings, as well as a few specimens of his simple tender hymns. "We are grateful to Mrs. Oliphant for a book of much interest and pathetic beauty, a book which none can read without being the better for it."—John Bull.

Pioneers and Founders; or, Recent Workers in the Mission Field. By CHARLOTTE M. YONGE, Author of "The Heir of Redclyffe." With Frontispiece, and Vignette Portrait of BISHOP HEBER.

The author has endeavoured in these narratives to bring together such of the more distinguished Missionaries of the English and American Nations as might best illustrate the character and growth of Mission-work in the last two centuries. The object has been to throw together such biographies as are most complete, most illustrative, and have been found most inciting to stir up others—representative lives, as far as possible. The missionaries whose biographies are here given, are—John Eliot, the Apostle of the Red Indians; David Brainerd, the Enthusiast; Christian F. Schwartz, the Councillor of Tanjore; Henry Martyn, the Scholar-Missionary; William Carey and Joshua Marshman, the Serampore Missionaries; the Judson Family; the Bishops of Calcutta,—Thomas Middleton, Reginald Heber, Daniel Wilson; Samuel Marsden, the Australian Chaplain and Friend of the Maori; John Williams, the Martyr of Erromango; Allen Gardener, the Sailor Martyr; Charles Frederick Mackenzie, the Martyr of Zambesi. "Likely to be one of the most popular of the 'Sunday Library' volumes."—Literary Churchman.

Angelique Arnauld, Abbess of Port Royal. By FRANCES MARTIN. Crown 8vo. 4s. 6d.

This new volume of the 'Sunday Library' contains the life of a very remarkable woman founded on the best authorities. She was a Roman Catholic Abbess who lived more than 200 years ago, whose life contained much struggle and suffering. But if we look beneath the surface, we find that sublime virtues are associated with her errors, there is something admirable in everything she does, and the study of her history leads to a continual enlargement of our own range of thought and sympathy. It is believed the volume is not surpassed in interest by any other belonging to this well-known series.

THE "BOOK OF PRAISE" HYMNAL,

COMPILED AND ARRANGED BY

SIR ROUNDELL PALMER,

In the following four forms:—
A. Beautifully printed in Royal 32mo., limp cloth, price 6d.
B.   ,,   ,,   Small 18mo., larger type, cloth limp, 1s.
C. Same edition on fine paper, cloth, 1s. 6d.
Also an edition with Music, selected, harmonized, and composed by **JOHN HULLAH**, in square 18mo., cloth, 3s. 6d.

The large acceptance which has been given to "The Book of Praise" by all classes of Christian people encourages the Publishers in entertaining the hope that this Hymnal, which is mainly selected from it, may be extensively used in Congregations, and in some degree at least meet the desires of those who seek uniformity in common worship as a means towards that unity which pious souls yearn after, and which our Lord prayed for in behalf of his Church. "The office of a hymn is not to teach controversial Theology, but to give the voice of song to practical religion. No doubt, to do this, it must embody sound doctrine; but it ought to do so, not after the manner of the schools, but with the breadth, freedom, and simplicity of the Fountain-head." On this principle has Sir R. Palmer proceeded in the preparation of this book.

The arrangement adopted is the following:—

PART I. *consists of Hymns arranged according to the subjects of the Creed*—"*God the Creator,*" "*Christ Incarnate,*" "*Christ Crucified,*" "*Christ Risen,*" "*Christ Ascended,*" "*Christ's Kingdom and Judgment,*" *etc.*

PART II. *comprises Hymns arranged according to the subjects of the Lord's Prayer.*

PART III. *Hymns for natural and sacred seasons.*

There are 320 Hymns in all.

CAMBRIDGE:—PRINTED BY J. PALMER.

www.ingramcontent.com/pod-product-compliance
Lightning Source LLC
Chambersburg PA
CBHW021824230426

43669CB00008B/857